For Alex, Lu, and Ezequiel Powell
In memory of Roneil Powell

The Violet Bakery Cookbook

Claire Ptak

Foreword by Alice Waters

Photography Kristin Perers

Ten Speed Press
Berkeley

Foreword

When Claire came to me many years ago and told me she would be leaving Chez Panisse to move to England, I had a whole landscape of feelings: sadness, of course, to be losing her wonderful spirit and talent, and a touch of jealousy that London would be gaining it; tremendous curiosity to see what she would do next; and confidence that whatever she might choose to do or make, it would be beautiful. And, indeed, Claire's Violet bakery, a modest little building just off London Fields in Hackney, is just that: a place of beauty. As soon as you walk into Violet you are won over by Claire's aesthetic—from the antique glass case brimming with her irresistible cakes to the leafy branches and heirloom roses she arranges in buckets throughout the shop, to a pile of blushing quince soon to be transformed into one of her exquisite fruit galettes. Violet is a place that feels a little like the kitchen of Chez Panisse, especially in the early years when we used to serve breakfast. The cooks work in an open kitchen and the smells wafting from their ovens warm the atmosphere in the tiny shop. Upstairs, customers sit unhurried with a cappuccino and an almond-cornmeal breakfast cake or a slice of Claire's beautifully reimagined Victoria sponge cake—Violet is a little corner of Northern California in east London.

I always knew that just because Claire was relocating to another continent, she wouldn't escape the Chez Panisse family! As I write this, I am still basking in the memory of two things that Claire made the other night, at a fundraiser for the Edible Schoolyard Project at Clarke's Restaurant. First, the most exquisite baked Alaska—I think the best I've had in my life! It was spectacular: raspberry ripple ice cream, the softest meringue ever (no one makes a meringue like Claire), a wonderful sponge cake. And then with the same effortlessness, she made a perfect rustic apple tart (page 174); though I have had versions of it at Chez Panisse countless times before, this one was radical in its simplicity, allowing the flavor of the English Chegworth Beauty apples to shine through.

One of the things I love most about Claire's palate is her unerring sense of balance. When it comes to sugar in her desserts, the sweetness never overwhelms or cloys. She keeps the flavors up there on this incredible tightrope. And she's able to do that because she is always asking herself the questions that matter: What does the new apple harvest taste like? How does spelt flour compare to buckwheat? Is this batch better than the last one I made? She is always searching for how to do it better the next time, never relying on the crutch of the familiar and the predictable. That kind of self-inquiry separates a good cook from a great one.

This is a lovely book to fall into. Just flipping through the pages, you instantly get a sense of Violet bakery: these aren't elaborately constructed creations from a big commercial kitchen or restaurant, but homey, delicious, nourishing things, full of heart and life and flavor. Claire's respect for the purity and simplicity of her ingredients comes across beautifully in both her recipes and evocative photographs: in the pristine loganberries, for example, freshly harvested from a local farm and tucked into the layers of a birthday cake; or in the craggy surface of a scone, broken in half and adorned with a slick of almond butter.

As you thumb through these wonderful images and recipes, you feel welcomed into Claire's kitchen in the most natural of ways. Her nuanced approach to season and place, sweet and savory, flavor and health, is what makes this book so special: it is about food that is lovingly crafted, always mindful of what is delicious, pure, and satisfying in the truest sense.

Alice Waters

"Many people will tell you they don't eat sweets. Do not believe them; in our experience, when these eclectics are confronted with some delicious pudding or pie they will set to it with the best."

Lord Westbury and Donald Downes, *With Gusto and Relish*, 1957

Contents

12. *Introduction*
42. *Morning*
74. *Midday*
102. *Afternoon*
156. *Evening*
196. *Party party*
224. *The Violet pantry*
256. *Notes on foraging*
260. *Index*

Recipe list

MORNING

Buns
58. Bacon and egg buttermilk biscuits
61. Cinnamon buns
72. Yellow peach crumb bun

Cereal
44. Quinoa, hazelnut, and
   cherry granola

Muffins
48. Apricot and almond-cornmeal
   muffins
57. Sweet potato, coconut, date,
   and rye muffins
64. Raspberry and star anise
   crumble muffins

Pudding
66. Chocolate croissant bread pudding

Scones
46. Prune, oat, and spelt scones
52. Blueberry, spelt, and oat scones
54. Buckwheat, apple, and crème
   fraîche scones
69. Strawberry, ginger, and poppy
   seed scones
70. Ham, cheese, and leek scones

MIDDAY

Bread puddings
78. Lacinato kale, leek, and ricotta
   bread pudding
96. Braised fennel, olive, and caper
   bread pudding

Quiches and tarts
82. Tomato and marjoram tarts
83. Mozzarella, rosemary,
   and new potato tarts

86. Squash, brown butter,
   and sage quiche
100. Sweet corn and roasted cherry
   tomato quiche

Savory buns
88. Chipotle and cheddar corn muffins
90. Sour cream, chive, and feta scones

Toasties
77. Cheddar and green onion toastie
   with quince jelly
95. Comté and chutney toastie

AFTERNOON

Cookies and bars
108. Buckwheat butter cookies
116. Nutty chocolate Barbados biscuits
120. Oatmeal and candied peel cookies
123. Chocolate oat agave cookies
133. Mandarin, ginger, and rye shards
134. Chewy ginger snaps
140. Egg yolk chocolate chip cookies
143. The Violet butterscotch blondie
144. Chocolate sandwich cookies
150. Kamut, vanilla, and chocolate
   chip cookies
153. Rye chocolate brownies
154. Coconut macaroons

Tart
130. Wild blackberry crumble tart

Tea and loaf cakes
104. Banana buttermilk bread
107. Coffee cardamom walnut cakes
110. Apricot kernel upside-down cake
114. Lemon drizzle loaf
118. Red plum Victoria sponge

125. Ginger molasses cake

126. Honey and rose water madeleines

128. Cream scones

137. Summer spelt almond cake

138. Olive oil sweet wine cake

149. Pistachio, hazelnut, and
    raspberry friands

EVENING

Cakes

187. Chocolate, prune, and
    whiskey cake

193. Chocolate sunken soufflé cake

Desserts

158. Summer pudding

160. Rhubarb galette

165. Rum babas

174. Alice Waters's apple galette

178. Cherry cobbler

181. Roasted black figs

188. Coconut cream trifle cake

Ices

161. Plum petal ice cream

170. Walnut praline ice cream

177. Melon granita

180. Fig leaf ice cream

184. Quince ice cream

PARTY PARTY

Cakes

199. Chocolate devil's food cake

204. Grandma Ptak's red velvet cake

208. Hazelnut toffee cake

213. Loganberry-vanilla birthday cake

219. Carrot cake

Icings

200. Salted caramel icing

203. Fragola grape icing

207. Coconut milk icing

216. Loganberry icing

217. Cream cheese icing

222. Violet icing

222. Marshmallow icing

THE VIOLET PANTRY

General

228. Vanilla extract

229. Spices

233. Candied citrus peel

234. Candied angelica

237. Salted caramel sauce

238. Caramel shards

241. Roasted quince

242. Frangipane

Jams

230. Quince jelly

245. Rhubarb and angelica jam

246. Apricot and pineapple sage jam

249. Peach and peach leaf jam

250. Strawberry and lemon
    verbena jam

253. Loganberry and geranium jam

254. Plum and tonka jam

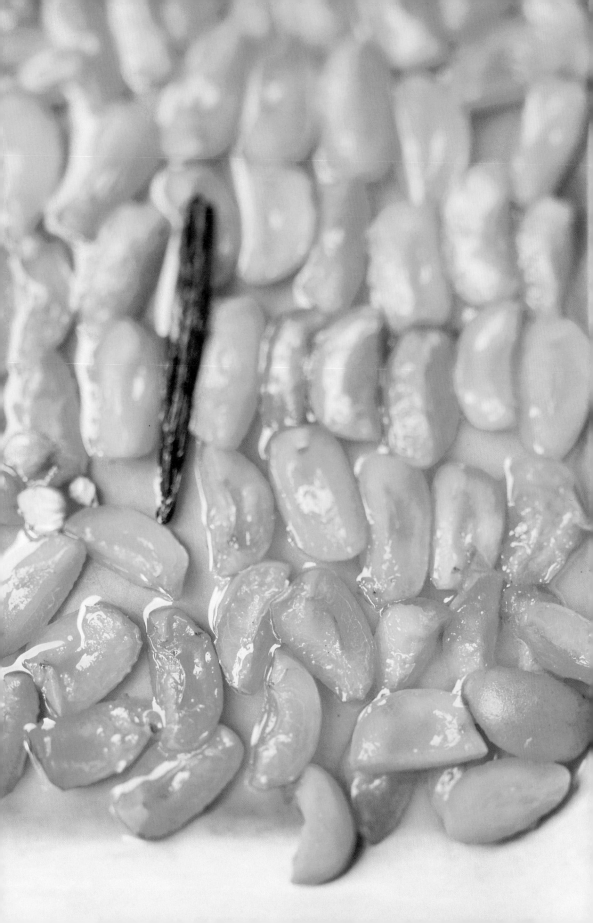

Introduction

To me, it's important that a cake be worth it, so taste is paramount. It has to be worth all the effort you have gone through making it, and of course it must be worth the calories. Eating cake involves a certain degree of guilt, let's be honest. We are conscious now more than ever of the dangers of too much sugar in our diets, and most of us are not only aware of our health but our weight too. More and more people are discovering valid food intolerances but still crave the treats they love. At Violet I have always been interested in baking with less sugar and the purest ingredients. Portions are substantial but not exaggerated. I bake primarily for taste—the most important part of any baking or cooking. If you are going to treat yourself, it had better be good, right? The aesthetic and presentation of my cakes are secondary. Often baking is approached from the other way around. While I do care a great deal about what my baked goods look like—and presentation is a huge part of what I do—I am most interested in creating something that tastes transcendent.

Just as you need to adjust your tomato sauce according to the strength of flavors in the tomatoes, so too you need to adjust your Victoria sponge according to the sweetness of the jam. An intensely concentrated and sweet strawberry jam will want a whipped cream that is not sweetened at all. Yet a tart lemon curd or rhubarb filling may need a lightly sweetened vanilla whipped cream to accompany it between the layers of sponge. Letting go of the worries about how scientific or difficult it is to bake, and approaching it with the same tools with which you might approach cooking, can make you more relaxed and, in turn, better equipped to use seasonal ingredients, less likely to waste food, and more inspired to create something that makes you proud.

The training I received from the chefs and cooks who I worked with at Chez Panisse was based entirely on making ingredients taste more like themselves, or the best version of themselves—coaxing out nuances in flavor by adding *sugar, salt, acid,* and *booze* or *extracts* to bring the dish perfectly into balance. A finished dish might need the addition of cream to balance out its tartness, or crème fraîche to save a too-rich

chocolate cake. Each day we baked, tasted, tweaked, and tasted again. I learned to approach sweet cooking the way a savory cook would. One way to understand this is to make ice cream, because with ice cream, you have a basic recipe for the base that usually has a combination of eggs and dairy to which you add a flavor, be it fruit, chocolate, caramel—the possibilities are endless. But once you make the recipe, you must taste the unfrozen base for balance of flavor. At this point you can make small adjustments with dramatically different results. But I am getting ahead of myself.

Home Baker

I never set out to start a bakery. I went to college to be a filmmaker. But the reality was that after classes and before going to see films, you would find me in the kitchen, baking. I once even baked in a borrowed oven on an island in Lake Atitlan in Guatemala, so strong was the urge to bake. I made apple pies and French baguettes for a group of backpackers and a crazy exiled Cuban artist who called the pie "Orgasmico!"

My parents and grandparents taught me how to cook. Food was at the center of our lives and signified joy. It was how we celebrated accomplishment and how we coped with loss. We were always in the kitchen helping and always foraging for the best wild and backyard produce. My parents are educators and writers, and although we were well taken care of, I watched my parents put in very long hours and struggle at times to pay the bills. Although I am sure they would have preferred to be more financially secure, it was an incredible motivator for me and my brother.

When I finished my studies, I worked as an assistant to a Hollywood director for one year, and all the while felt something was missing. I then took a year off and worked in the San Francisco boutique Metier, selling my favorite clothes and incredible diamond jewelery. I longed to afford the styles. We girls would leave work and head to Urban Outfitters for the knock-offs and spend days off thrift-store and vintage shopping. Sheri, our amazing boss, took us on a yearly thank-you trip to the California Wine Country, where we got to experience its famous restaurants. I became more and more drawn to the idea of cooking professionally, and was encouraged by my friends and colleagues to pursue it. In 2001 I went for a one-day internship at Chez Panisse.

In those days, people tended to stay at one restaurant for much longer—ten-, fifteen-, twenty-year veterans were teaching me at Chez—and I thought if I could swing getting a job there too, then that was it. Career sorted. Although they wanted to hire me right away, no one ever left. The first opening in the pastry department came a year later, when I was about to move to London. But my dream job called and so I answered and figured everything else out later.

Chez Panisse
Alice Waters pulled me aside in the kitchen of Chez Panisse one day toward the end of my years there and whispered in her mellifluous voice, "We NEED to talk." I knew my path was about to change, but I didn't know how. In the three years I had worked in the pastry department of Chez Panisse, my interactions with Alice had been few and far between. Although she was at the restaurant nearly every day, and tasted my cooking frequently, her comments were usually fed through one of the chefs, or the general manager. With more than 100 employees, and newly forged relationships with presidents, teachers, artists, intellectuals, and farmers occupying her time, she wasn't always available for a chat.

Since I had begun working at the restaurant, I lived and breathed nothing but preparing, tasting, and reading about food and how to make it taste as good as possible. Under the then pastry chef Alan Tangren, I learned how to taste. We tested every single thing we made every single day. He taught me to

navigate the line between simplicity and intricacy, and he taught me to know when to stop. And he was crazy when it came to walnuts. According to Alan, who learned under Chez Panisse's founding pastry chef, Lindsey Shere, walnuts should never really be toasted but only just barely warmed through and taken to where they only just begin to color and release their oils. Using your senses in the kitchen is crucial. When you get that first warm whiff of walnut emanating from the oven, he told me, the nuts are ready.

The time I spent in the kitchen at Chez Panisse was undistracted. My English boyfriend, Damian, had moved back to London to study just as I was hired, and while I missed him terribly, it allowed me to focus. The eight-hour time difference meant that when I finished plating desserts for the downstairs restaurant at midnight, I could phone him in England while he was having his breakfast. I remember well these thirty- to forty-minute calls (pre-Skype, I had memorized a twenty-plus-digit international calling card number). Me, after a gratifying but exhausting service filling 300 profiteroles with mulberry ice cream (and my after-shift glass of wine), sitting in my car parked outside the restaurant; him, with a cup of strong English tea and toasted Poilâne sourdough, preparing for class.

But after those three years apart, Damian and I were ready to resume where we had left off and live together. This time, in London. Alice pulled me aside that day to ask me—point-blank—not to leave. She understood I wanted to follow my heart, but she wanted me to think of all the things I could do if I stayed at Chez Panisse. My role would be more significant. The pay would be better. I was filled with butterflies, and so conflicted. But paradoxically, her belief in me only gave me greater confidence to leave. I was determined to follow my heart and to live in London, where the restaurants were just starting a small revolution of their own. Markets were burgeoning and cooks were cooking in such a different way. Plus, Paris was only a three-hour train journey away. Alice understood completely. She gave me her blessing and said she would see me in London as her daughter, Fanny, would be studying at Cambridge. Ten years later, as an experienced business owner, I know first-hand what it is like to lose a valuable cook. You will do almost anything to keep them, but you also know they ought to spread their wings.

But as Alice taught me and as I tell all my deserters, "You can always come back!"

Food Styling

When I got to London, I did stages at some of my favorite restaurants. Staging is one of the wonderful perks of working in the industry. It is like being part of a private club—you go to any restaurant where there are similar values and mutual respect among the owners and chefs and work in their kitchen for a short time. St. John Restaurant was my introduction to the wonderful world of British puddings. I never knew how good raisins, prunes, treacle, and caraway seeds were! St. John blew my mind, and to this day is one of my favorite places in the world to eat a sweet treat. The wonderful Spanish and North African–inspired Moro was my next stage, where I was introduced to the delicious cooking of Southern Spain and North Africa, leading me to travel to Granada and Marrekesh in search of these flavors. Next I worked for a brief time at The Anchor and Hope and answered phones at The River Café. I was amazed to learn that almost nobody had a position for a dedicated pastry chef. The cooks did all the baking (save for at St. John) and, while I loved savory food and was already an accomplished cook, my heart was in the cakes. The stages were enlightening, but as much as I loved them, I realized I wanted a break from restaurants.

I had met Jamie Oliver in California through mutual friends, and he asked me to contact him when I got to London. He then introduced me to his team of food stylists and I worked with them on a couple of his projects as well as assisting them on other freelance jobs, learning the ins and outs of styling food for the camera. But most of the stylists I assisted were not cooks. They were incredibly talented creatives. The food styling rule at the time was that if you wear an apron or make the food taste too good, you are only a glorified housekeeper. Pretty soon they will be asking you to make tea and wanting to know when lunch is ready. It was up to us to make food styling a profession—to lift it out of the ranks of home economics. But the cook in me couldn't bear to leave out the salt.

The Californian in me couldn't bear to waste all that food. So instead, I cooked and tasted and seasoned and kept learning. I longed to make the food we were making that looked so

beautiful taste better. I taught myself how to make all this food look beautiful by gently caring for and lifting the dish out of the realm of just a rote, cooked recipe. I always season the food I cook for photographs because I think if it actually tastes good, it will look better.

After about a year, I stopped assisting and started doing my own food styling. I was invited to bake a cake for Simon Hopkinson's reissue of *The Prawn Cocktail Years*. The cake was to be shot by Jason Lowe at Simon's west London flat. The cake was a Black Forest gateau made of ganache and whipped cream and kirsch-soaked black cherries. I made the cake twice to be sure it was perfect, then packed it up and took the Tube there. When I arrived at Simon's peaceful book-filled home, a rice pudding was in the oven and the griddle was heating up for steak with bone marrow. A bottle of 1974 Robert Mondavi Reserve was breathing on the table. Jason photographed the cake, the steaks, and the rice pudding, and then we had them all for lunch. Beautiful food that was unsurpassed in flavor. Simon was cooking for the camera AND for us. It was a revelation.

Then came Yotam Ottolenghi's weekly column in the *Guardian*. I started to style his food in 2007. He wrote a vegetarian column, and at that time he was not known outside London. His recipes spoke to me, and their flavors were so daring and different from what I had cooked before. We joked that it was "flavor crazy," but in a good way. Tart, sour, sweet, creamy, and satisfying cooking grounded in the flavors of Israel and peppered with the familiarity of Mediterranean and British cooking.

Broadway Market
Simultaneously with the food styling, I was secretly planning my own bakery business. My now-husband and I lived in a large one-bedroom flat in a converted schoolhouse in east London. It was open-plan with a relatively large kitchen. I did my research and found that, with a few licences and certificates and my meager savings of about £1,000, I could bake from home and start a cottage industry selling at the newly resurrected Broadway Market in Hackney.

It took three months of phone calls, meetings, and appointments with the council to get through the red tape and into the market, so my first day there felt like such a triumph. I baked

until about two in the morning, and then woke up at six to finish icing cakes, bake off my apple galettes (page 174), and pack up the car. Bundled up in multiple layers to protect against the damp November cold, I arrived at the market on the urban tumbleweed of a road. Iron-framed market stalls were already there, but you had to place the chipboard tabletops yourself. I unfolded my crisply ironed white tablecloth and looked around at the empty marketplace. I suddenly felt very American. I was so clean and tidy and overeager.

Nobody really came to Broadway Market back then, except the cooks and artisans themselves, and a handful of local residents who really understood what was going on. But slowly the market started to grow in popularity and so my business grew too. I remember my first regulars: one couple came to the stall every Saturday to buy one single slice of ginger molasses cake, split between two. They never said a word, just passed me their chosen slice, handed me a few coins, and waited for me to bag up and pass back their slice. They have come nearly every weekend since, for almost ten years. It is these interactions that make a community.

Wilton Way

Over the years the stall outgrew itself. I expanded into two stalls side by side, but I couldn't meet the demands for my cakes while cooking out of my home kitchen, so Damian and I started looking for a commercial kitchen space. We finally found Violet's home on Wilton Way. It was very run-down, and an artist was using the exterior as his canvas. I desperately needed more room to bake for the market and thought I could transform this space. Somehow. Plus, the price was right. At first, it was not my intention to open up a shop. But as soon as it got a lick of paint and the oven and mixer arrived, people from the neighborhood were knocking on the door asking if we were opening a Violet bakery. Damian and I looked at each other and said, "Um, yes!"

Violet is on an unassuming residential street near London Fields park in Hackney, east London. It is a freestanding off-white stucco building that reminds me more of the architecture of California than of England. A mural sign painted down one side of the building is based on a Latin American and California-Mexican vibe. It was different from my already well-established logo, but it fitted the building. Inside, my 500-square-foot space with dairy-white walls and natural woodwork is now a bustling bakery and café. My husband makes playlists that we listen to while we work and that the customers seem to love too. I sometimes think we are getting as well known for our playlists as for our cakes.

My bakers work on a 1949 green Hobart mixer and a white enamel gas range that I repurposed from an old hospital. My lovely staff of young, flour-dusted bakers are always busy at work producing impossible numbers of cinnamon buns, scones, muffins, cupcakes, cookies, whoopie pies, and layer cakes out of the teensy space. A vintage wooden-and-glass men's shirt display case was refurbished for our cake case. It is always filled to the brim and on weekends it literally overflows onto the counter.

The Cakes

When I started my stall, I baked only my favorite cakes, tarts, galettes, and scones. I thought it best to start with what I was really good at, what my friends and family had already approved of, and what I myself loved to eat. I quickly learned why they call it market research. Selling at an open market directly to your customers is amazing. You find out exactly what people do and don't like and why. It is a great way to start a business. Just as our tastes for fashion, design, and architecture change, so do our tastes for food. The cupcake is the perfect example. While the cupcake will always be (when made well) the perfectly proportioned marriage of cake and frosting, it is now somewhat out of fashion. The market tells us this quite clearly. We went from making a few dozen to hundreds per week to thousands

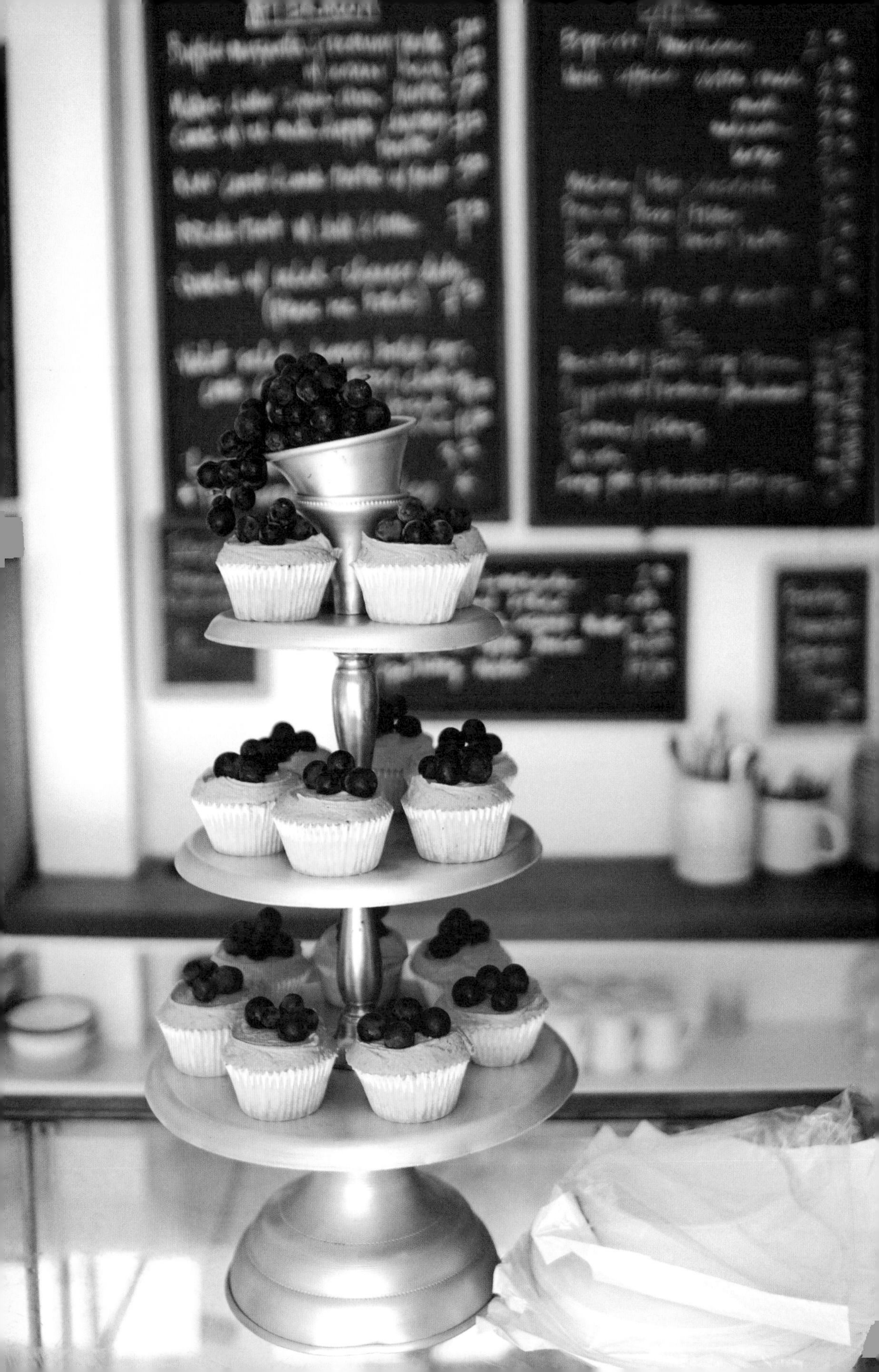

per week and back down to hundreds per week. Truthfully, this makes me happy, because it creates more space for all of the other wonderful cakes out there that I long to make at Violet.

In the last few years I have become increasingly interested in alternatives to processed wheat and sugar and dairy from cows. I have been experimenting a lot with whole grains and unrefined sugars. Having been asked to write my first cookbook on confectionary, I did months of research on sugars and how best to boil them down into those old-time sweets. I wrote over 120 recipes with sugar as the main ingredient. I tested them all and then made them again for the photographs for the book. All the while I tasted and tweaked and got them just right. The bad news was, that after making hundreds of pieces of candy, I made myself ill. I was experiencing headaches and sluggishness and exhaustion. I cut all of it out completely for two months and cleansed my system. At that point I started to have much more sympathy for those with intolerances to gluten, sugar, and dairy. I wanted to create recipes for those people as well as people just taking a break or cutting back. But I wanted these recipes to taste fantastic. I have added many of them to the menu at Violet and they are chronicled on these pages too.

I have also come to realize that there are two palates of sweet. One is better satisfied by a treacle-, caramel-, or toffee-based dessert. The other prefers fruit- and pastry-based desserts that are often served with cream or just eaten on their own. Luckily for my business, my husband and I fall into these separate categories. So he pulls me back when I want to make everything fruit based and reminds me that the toffee lovers of the world are feeling neglected. My own palate calls for growing my own lemon verbena, rosemary, mint, and rose geranium in pots in our back seating area at Violet. I add herbs to our quick strawberry jam; the pears from the tree in the neighboring council estate are picked and poached and turned into tarts. Fig leaves foraged from the Hackney area infuse our custards and enhance the flavor of our figs when we roast them to put in our Apricot and Almond-Cornmeal Muffins (page 48). For his palate, we caramelize sugar with vanilla pods and add butter and salt in the final stages. Day-old Cinnamon Buns (page 61) are turned into fluffy, custardy bread pudding with added cardamom.

The pleasure of waiting for strawberries to come back into season and the anticipation each year of the elusive apricot inspire us in the kitchen at Violet. In the spring, colors burst and we capture bright yellows by using puréed Alphonso mangos as our base; in the summer and early fall, it's pinks and deep purples from raspberries, black currants, and then fragola grapes; finally, in the winter, we have white citrusy icings, snowy coconut, and bright pink forced rhubarb. We don't need any food coloring (except of course in Grandma Ptak's Red Velvet Cake, page 204) because the fruits are already giving us the color. To us at Violet, these simple methods seem fresher and more current than ever.

Mise en place

In my first performance review at Chez Panisse I was called out for not setting up my mise en place well enough; something, I was told, I had to improve. I was slowing down the other chefs and running the risk of making mistakes. I was devastated. I had bad mise en place? It was so embarrassing. My lack of training was starting to show and I felt self-conscious about it. Pre-iPhone, I had to go home and look it up.

Mise en place is the French term for having everything in its place in the kitchen. It is a good idea to have your mise en place ready for each recipe in this book before you begin it. It will save time and confusion and make you a more organized and better cook and baker. I recommend you start by reading the entire recipe all the way through, twice. Then measure each ingredient out into small bowls (or teacups or any other containers you have) before you start mixing anything together. This way, you are much less likely to leave out ingredients or mix the wrong ingredients together. I heeded the advice and now drill it into my own cooks. *Mise en place, mise en place, mise en place!!*

AERATING. Any time you are working with a mixture that relies on the incorporation of air (and therefore the task of keeping that air inside the mixture) you will want to work quickly. So a proper mise en place will help you immensely. This includes separating and whipping eggs, with or without sugar, before folding them into other ingredients.

When beating butter and sugar for cakes, I like to take it to the max. This means creaming butter and sugar in a stand mixer with a paddle attachment until it doubles in volume and becomes pale and fluffy. Start with softened butter.

When beating butter and sugar for cookies, I ease off a little. I like my cookies slightly chewy and gooey on the inside and crisp on the outside. I think a cake should be a cake and a cookie should be a cookie. So when you beat the butter and sugar for your chocolate chip cookies, for example, simply mix them well together without incorporating too much air, otherwise the air trapped in the butter will be released in the cookie, making it

soft and cakey. The less air, the crisper the cookie. Ever noticed how your cookies are perfect the day they are baked but then go soft the next day? To remedy this, put the baked cookies on a baking sheet lined with parchment paper and warm them through in the oven. The heat of the oven will cause the moisture that the cookies have absorbed from the atmosphere to evaporate, making them crisp again.

DRY INGREDIENTS. Rather than sifting, I prefer to whisk my dry ingredients together. It means less washing up, it is faster, and, in most cases, it does the trick. Occasionally my recipes will require you to sift ingredients such as confectioners' sugar in order to avoid those annoying lumps.

FOOD PROCESSOR. A food processor or immersion blender is a wonderful tool that can rescue a recipe when a mixture splits or has lumps. For instance, confectioners' sugar can sometimes get lumpy in our moist, rainy climate; when a little moisture gets into the sugar, the sugar tends to clump. So if you rush things and skip the sifting, or if sifting doesn't do enough, then put the sugar in a food processor to get the lumps out. Likewise, if you find lumps in your buttercream that you hadn't noticed earlier, simply process the buttercream until smooth. This knocks the air out, so, afterward, pop the buttercream back into the mixer and use the paddle attachment for 3 minutes on a lowish speed to whip it up again.

WEIGHING VERSUS MEASURING. At Violet we weigh everything, and I suggest you do this at home too. Cup measures can vary greatly and it's important to be precise in baking. If you haven't got one already, I recommend you invest in a small digital kitchen scale. Most allow you to switch back and forth between grams and ounces, which means you can use cookbooks from around the world, converting from imperial to metric, or vice versa.

CAKE PANS. I like to bake a layer cake in a single deep cake pan— at least 7.5cm (3 inches) deep—and then cut the cake into layers. But if you prefer to bake the individual layers in separate layer pans, you can do this too. It's just that I find you don't get as much lift on the sides of the cake when baking in shallower layer pans.

MELTED BUTTER. At Violet, we melt a little panful of butter to use for greasing our baking pans. We simply brush the insides of the pans with the melted butter for quick and even greasing. This enables us to get right into the corners and not leave any spots that could cause unwanted sticking later.

Tasting notes

At Violet we use sugars, salts, acids, boozes, and extracts to balance the four basic tastes of *sweet, salt, bitter,* and *sour* in order to get balance. This is nothing new or groundbreaking, but I don't think we usually think about balancing flavor in baking like we do in cooking. Yet, it is essential to good baking. It is probably responsible for the sudden surge in salted caramel or sea salt chocolate. The salt makes the taste more balanced, more palatable, and therefore more enjoyable.

SWEET. Sugar is the subject of much controversy. I am going to neither denigrate it nor praise it here. We all know that you shouldn't have too much of it, but that when you do use it, it can be the ultimate treat. It is what makes up the comfort foods associated with grandmothers and birthdays and weddings. It marks the end of a great meal, and it gets you through an afternoon when you start flagging. Sugar is a wonderful way to heighten flavor. I am not trying to make something sweet, in fact I much prefer cakes that are less sweet. I am trying to bring out the flavors inherent in the cakes (fruit, chocolate, nuts) by adding sugar so that the ingredients taste more like themselves. I am trying to bring out their essence. Balancing the amount of sugar that goes into baking is more important than you might think. The addition or subtraction of a tablespoon of sugar can be very significant in a dessert or baked goods. The sugar can overpower, as we all know, but it can also bring the flavor of something into bloom, much in the same way salt makes savory food more delicious. It brings to the fore the purity of an ingredient's natural flavor. A salted avocado shouldn't taste salty, just more like an avocado.

SALT. Salt is increasingly popular in sweet preparations. Salted caramel, for example, has become nearly as popular a flavor as chocolate. I remember when I first served a salted caramel cupcake at my stall in 2005. Many of my new customers eyed me with suspicion. Salt? In a cupcake? They were either puzzled or repulsed by the idea. But after gentle encouragement that the

salt acted only as a way to balance the sweetness of the caramel, I began to win them over. The French have been doing it for ages, but the Americans came to it much later, and the British (I'm sorry to say) later still. At the time I started Violet, the salt and caramel flavor combination started to sweep the nation. Now you can find salted caramel everything, including scented candles, which I am not sure is necessarily a good thing.

Salt can actually cancel out bitter flavors, so that what our taste buds register is something altogether different. We add a pinch of salt to our bitter hot chocolate at Violet, because the salt makes the hot chocolate drink taste sweeter without having to add more sugar. No one thinks it's strange anymore to add a pinch of salt to a sweet dish. But aside from the overt salty flavor in a salted caramel, trace amounts of salt have always been used in sweet dishes to balance sweetness. Salt is a wonderful tool in the savory kitchen to season and boost flavor. The sweet kitchen benefits from its ability to elicit the true nature of a combination of ingredients just as much as the savory kitchen.

BITTER. Coffee is the backbone of my business at Violet. It has been a bit of a journey to get right. Making a perfect espresso coffee on a proper machine with expertly roasted beans can be as difficult and satisfying as making a perfect cake. I say coffee is the backbone of my business because we could not survive financially without it. Much like a restaurant needs to sell alcohol to turn a profit on food, we have to sell a lot of coffee to make a profit on cake. But the other side to this is that the bitterness of coffee goes very well with the sweetness of cake. More developed palates tend to prefer bitter flavors. Chocolate, grapefruit peel, marmalade, coffee, and alcohol are some of the bitter flavors we use often at Violet. As I mentioned above, salt masks the bitter flavor, so a very bitter dark caramel or dark chocolate loves a little salt. Our oatmeal cookies (page 120) have candied grapefruit peel in them, which balances with the sweetness of this lacey cookie, and a pinch of salt helps to balance the bitterness of the grapefruit added. And so a perfect cookie is born.

Vanilla is also a good mask for bitterness. Some of the whole grain flours that I use have a slightly bitter edge to them.

Buckwheat, spelt, and rye are all slightly bitter. The addition of vanilla to the recipes that call for these flours is a great way to pull them into balance.

Booze falls into the bitter-balancing category, though alcohol in desserts and baking has something of a bad name. The chocolate box at our house was never around for long, but no one ever touched the brandied cherry confections. They were too sweet, too strong, and too bland, all at once. Admittedly they probably were not the most expensive chocolates available, but they supported their bad reputation. However, a boozy dessert can be just the thing to finish a meal. And a little splash of booze can be used as another flavor-balancing tool. I love using a couple of spoonfuls of rum in coconut frosting or a little Cointreau or Grand Marnier with blood orange or clementine cakes. There are some really interesting eaux de vie and fruit brandies being produced now that complement so many different fruits. I particularly like a quince liqueur made in England by Bramley and Gage.

SOUR. Acid levels greatly influence the balance of flavor in baking. Lemon juice is the one we use most often, but acid also comes from acidic fruits and jams. We prefer jams made with tarter fruits for our Cream Scones (page 128), for example. Rhubarb is a wonderful jam to balance the creamy and sweet nature of a scone. When making buttercream icing for our cakes and cupcakes, acid is a very important ingredient. The main composition is unsalted butter and confectioners' sugar, whipped to a creamy consistency with the addition of a flavoring. The flavoring could be a fruit purée, melted chocolate, or flavored milk. After the main flavor is added, I taste and adjust for flavor. Lemon juice plays a key role in cutting the creamy sweetness of the icing. Sometimes we serve half a grapefruit at Violet for breakfast. Rather than sprinkling it with sugar, I like to sprinkle a pinch of salt on it. This masks much of the sour taste of grapefruit and makes it seem sweeter without having to add sugar. Genius!

The recipes

This book delves deeply into the most important aspect of baking—flavor. Learning to work with fruits to better highlight their qualities may sound simple, but it is the minutiae of flavor balance that I find interesting. The recipes here also celebrate the caramel-sweet and chocolate palates, while perhaps giving new ideas about combining your favorite ingredients with whole grain flours, as in our awesome Rye Chocolate Brownies (page 153).

This book contains the recipes I have been developing and using over the past ten years: recipes most often requested by customers, friends, Instagram followers, Facebook likers, and readers of my *Guardian* blog posts. I am often asked by friends who are also cooks and chefs if I can help them with a recipe for, say, Rum Babas (page 165), cakes without wheat flour, or just a reliable, really flaky pastry (page 82). I have tried to include them all here. Some recipes you have seen before, while some are new and contain seldom-seen ingredients. I would love you to roll up your sleeves and try to bake them with an open mind and a clean palate. Taste what you are making and make it better. Trust your own instincts and don't be afraid to try something new.

BUTTER. At Violet we always bake with unsalted butter and we serve salted butter with toast. Unless otherwise stated, use unsalted butter for the recipes in the book.

SUGAR. We use pure superfine cane sugar in our recipes. The flavor and texture of cane sugar is different from (and preferable to) sugar made from sugar beets. Superfine sugar dissolves faster and is preferred for baking, but granulated also works well.

FINE SPELT FLOUR. You can sift the bran from whole grain spelt flour to get a fine spelt. Weigh or measure the flour after sifting.

PARCHMENT PAPER. We always line our baking pans with parchment paper to make it easier to remove the cakes.

OVEN TEMPERATURE. All ovens vary. The temperature is affected by how old it is, how full it is, and how many times you open it. Check your cakes for signs of doneness: smell, color, and springiness, and by inserting a skewer.

Morning

Mornings at Violet are my favorite time. I am a morning person; I always have been. I love anything baked in the morning for breakfast, and I would easily eat cake for breakfast every day if I didn't know any better. I do keep a jar of my quinoa granola at home and love to serve it with a good goat's or sheep's milk yogurt as much as with cow's milk yogurt. Many days I simply have a banana or a piece of sourdough or rye toast for my own breakfast. Sometimes it's a boiled egg. At Violet we serve generous slices of sourdough with salted butter, seasonal jam, and raw almond butter with sea salt. We get a cold-pressed almond butter from Cornwall that is so sweet and almondy that I prefer it to a toasted variety.

My favorite recipe in this section is possibly the cinnamon bun—a quick and easy bun that melts in your mouth. Every Sunday my friends Sylvia and Jo and I get cinnamon buns and coffees from the bakery and head up to Hackney Marshes with our dogs. A long walk in the wild fields that are also home to many of the ingredients I like to forage for is the perfect way to end the hectic London week.

The recipes in this section are a selection of breakfast items from across a year at Violet. I have included my favorite fruit and muffin or scone pairings from each season, but you can of course substitute here and there where appropriate, depending on what is best at the market.

Quinoa, hazelnut, and cherry granola

This is a gluten-free, refined sugar–free granola that is really crunchy, tart and warming. The pinch of salt brings it all together. The sour cherries go well with the sweetness of the agave and the warmth of toasted hazelnuts. Quinoa is ever so slightly bitter, so the salt mellows it and, together, this granola becomes something else. I have become a fan of sheep's milk yogurt lately and think it works really well as an accompaniment here.

Makes 1 extra-large jar

500g (6 cups) quinoa flakes

125g (1 cup) whole hazelnuts

50g (½ cup) ground flaxseeds

50g (⅓ cup) sesame seeds

50g (¾ cup) pumpkin seeds

50g (¼ cup) millet

290g (¾ cup plus 2 tablespoons) agave syrup

50g (3½ tablespoons) olive oil (not extra virgin)

100g (½ cup) coconut oil

100g (½ cup) water

1½ teaspoons vanilla extract

a few grates of fresh nutmeg

a pinch of sea salt

150g (1 cup) dried sour cherries, unsweetened if available

Preheat the oven to 150°C/300°F (130°C/265°F convection). Line two baking sheets or roasting pans with parchment paper.

Combine the quinoa flakes, whole hazelnuts, flaxseeds, sesame seeds, pumpkin seeds, and millet in a large bowl and set aside.

In a pan, combine the agave syrup, olive oil, coconut oil, and water. Place over medium heat and whisk constantly to melt it all together.

Remove the syrup mixture from the heat and stir in the vanilla, nutmeg, and sea salt. Pour this over the quinoa mixture and stir well to coat it completely.

Spread the mixture out on the lined baking sheets or roasting pans. Bake for 30 minutes. Remove from the oven, toss well with a metal spatula, and return to the oven. Lower the temperature to 140°C/285°F (120°C/250°F convection) and bake for another 30 minutes, turning every 10 minutes, until the mixture is golden.

Remove from the oven and allow to cool completely before stirring in the sour cherries. Store in an airtight container.

Prune, oat, and spelt scones

I got the idea for these scones after many a delicious bowl of porridge from the St. John Bread and Wine restaurant in London's Brick Lane. I didn't want to serve porridge at Violet, but I wanted those beautiful Earl Grey tea–soaked prunes and oats to start the day. These scones are basically a takeout version of porridge. Earl Grey tea is one of those ingredients that makes whatever you add it to taste more like itself, so here the prunes absorb the tea and taste, well, more pruney. It's remarkable. I recommend making the dough for these scones the night before and chilling it in the fridge. In the morning you can portion out the mixture and bake the scones fresh.

Makes 12 large scones

4 tablespoons brewed Earl Grey tea

300g (10½ ounces) pitted prunes

200g (2 cups) rolled oats,
  plus more for sprinkling on top

375g (3 cups plus 2 tablespoons)
  whole grain spelt flour

80g (½ cup) light brown sugar

1 tablespoon baking powder

1 teaspoon baking soda

1 teaspoon kosher salt

300g (1⅓ cups) cold unsalted butter,
  cut into 1cm (½ inch) cubes

2 egg yolks

2 eggs

4 tablespoons maple syrup

250g (1 cup) plain yogurt

1 egg beaten with 2 tablespoons
  milk, for the egg wash

Butter a 20 by 30-cm (8 by 12-inch) baking pan and line with parchment paper.

Pour the hot tea into a small bowl, put the pitted prunes in it, and set aside.

In a bowl, combine the oats, spelt flour, brown sugar, baking powder, baking soda, and salt, and whisk together. Use a pastry cutter or the back of a fork to cut the cubes of butter into the dry ingredients. You could also do this in a stand mixer. Mix together until it resembles coarse meal.

In another bowl, whisk together the yolks, eggs, maple syrup, and yogurt. Pour this into the dry ingredients and mix until just combined. Spoon the mixture into the prepared baking pan and spread it out. Tear the soaked prunes into bite-size pieces and dot on top. Push the prunes down into the mixture, then pour the remaining liquid from the soaked prunes over the top and spread flat with an icing spatula or rubber spatula. Cover with plastic wrap and chill for about 3 hours or overnight.

When ready to cook, preheat the oven to 200°C/390°F (180°C/355°F convection). Line a baking sheet with parchment paper.

Pop the chilled scone mixture out of the pan and cut into 12 triangles. Do this by cutting the block in half lengthwise. Cut each half into three squares and then cut each square into two triangles. (If you don't want to bake all the scones at this stage, just wrap them individually in plastic wrap and put whatever you don't want to bake in the freezer for future use. No need to defrost them before baking either. They bake right out of the freezer each time you want one.) Place the scones you want to bake on the lined baking sheet about 5cm (2 inches) apart. Brush the tops with the egg wash, sprinkle with the remaining oats, and bake for 35 to 40 minutes until golden. These are best eaten on the day you bake them.

Apricot and almond-cornmeal muffins

The almond-cornmeal muffin started its life as an upside-down cake. I wanted to produce a rich almondy cake that was both crumbly and moist. The cornmeal gives it that crumbly crunch while the almond paste gives it the oiliness of finely ground almonds that I find so appealing in a cake. I liked the idea that it would be made without wheat flour, but more for texture than principle. These muffins' best place is at the breakfast table, embellished with roasted fruits. Apricots, plums, quince, figs, and cherries are some of my favorites.

Makes 12 muffins

10 to 12 apricots

a sprinkle of sugar

250g (1 cup plus 1 tablespoon) unsalted butter, at room temperature

440g (15½ ounces) almond paste (a least 60 percent almonds), broken into pieces

125g (¼ cup plus 2 tablespoons) sugar

zest of 1 orange

3 eggs

2 teaspoons baking powder

½ teaspoon salt

225g (1¾ cups plus 2 tablespoons) fine cornmeal

First, prepare the fruit. Slice the apricots into quarters and toss in a bowl with a sprinkle of sugar. Set aside to macerate.

Preheat the oven to 190°C/375°F (170°C/340°F convection). Double-line a 12-cup muffin pan with paper liners. (I suggest using two liners per muffin because the fruit makes these particularly juicy.)

In a stand mixer, cream the butter, almond paste, sugar, and orange zest until pale and fluffy. Add the eggs slowly and mix well.

In a separate bowl, whisk together the baking powder, salt, and cornmeal. Add this to the butter mixture and mix well. Scoop into the lined muffin pan and press the pieces of fruit on top of the muffins.

Bake the muffins for about 30 minutes, until an inserted skewer comes out clean and the tops of the muffins spring back to the touch. Allow to cool for about 10 minutes before removing from the tin. These keep well for up to 4 days in an airtight container.

TASTE. For extra-luxurious muffins, roast the fruit first. Cut the fruit into quarters and place, cut side up, in a roasting pan. Sprinkle with sugar and a little water, and taste. Depending on the ripeness and the variety of the fruit, you may want to add half a scraped vanilla pod, the zest of 1 orange or lemon, or half a cinnamon stick. Roast for 35 to 45 minutes, until soft and a little caramelized. Use a bit more fruit as it shrinks in the cooking.

Blueberry, spelt, and oat scones

These scones can be served the English way for afternoon tea—split and filled with the compote and strained sheep's milk yogurt—or the American way, where they are served warm at breakfast with the compote or almond butter on the side. You could also just slather them with butter, although the idea for these scones came to me when I was taking a break from cow's dairy and refined sugars. I wanted to bake something that had the texture of a scone, but was lighter and with less gluten. If you want to go totally gluten free, you can substitute gluten-free flour for the whole grain spelt flour. If you are a vegan, then leave out the yogurt. If you don't have oat flour, pulverize rolled oats in the food processor.

Makes 12 scones

300g (2 cups) whole grain spelt flour, plus more for rolling

150g (1½ cups) oat flour

½ teaspoon kosher salt

1 teaspoon baking powder

1 teaspoon baking soda

50g (7 teaspoons) agave syrup

45g (5 teaspoons) maple syrup

100g (⅓ cup plus 1 tablespoon) freshly squeezed orange juice

1 tablespoon orange zest

4 heaped tablespoons (about 100g/3½ ounces) almond butter

100g (⅓ cup plus 2 tablespoons) coconut oil, melted

200g (1¾ cups) fresh blueberries

FOR THE COMPOTE

200g (1¾ cups) fresh blueberries

30g (4 teaspoons) agave syrup

TO SERVE

400g (1⅔ cups) sheep's milk yogurt, strained overnight

The day before you want to serve these, put your sheep's milk yogurt into a muslin-lined sieve or colander and rest over a bowl. Cover with plastic wrap and place in the fridge.

Line a baking sheet with parchment paper.

To make the scones, whisk together the spelt flour, oat flour, sea salt, baking powder, and baking soda in a bowl.

In another bowl, whisk together the agave and maple syrups, the orange juice and zest, and the almond butter. Pour in the melted coconut oil and whisk together.

Make a well in the middle of the dry ingredients and add the wet ingredients along with the blueberries. Mix until the wet and dry ingredients are just combined.

Allow the dough to rest for 5 minutes. Turn the dough out onto a lightly floured surface and roll it into a circle about 3.5-cm (1½-inch) thick. Use a 6-cm (2½-inch) cutter to cut out circles and place them on the lined baking sheet. Chill in the fridge while you make the compote.

Meanwhile, preheat your oven to 180°C/355°F (160°C/320°F convection).

To make the compote, put the berries and agave syrup into a small pan and cook gently until the berries start to burst. Continue to simmer for about 10 minutes, until the berries have become a little jammy. Take off the heat and allow to cool.

Bake the scones for 15 to 20 minutes until slightly golden. Serve immediately or allow to cool and then split in half. Spread a dollop of blueberry compote on one half and top with a spoonful of the strained yogurt. Place the other half on top and serve.

Buckwheat, apple, and crème fraîche scones

Buckwheat flour is one of my favorite flours to bake with. It has a very strong flavor, so it works best when mixed with other flours. It is also gluten free. In this recipe I've added a combination of spelt and oat flours to bolster the buckwheat. Spelt and oat are flavorful, but when mixed with buckwheat, they take a backseat. The spelt has enough gluten to carry the scones and yet leave them with a very appealing crumbly texture. The grated apple is sweet and moist and marries perfectly with the crème fraîche. For more on flours, read my pantry section (see page 224).

Makes 12 large scones

150g (1½ cups) fine spelt flour (see page 40), plus more for rolling

100g (⅔ cup) whole grain spelt flour

175g (1⅔ cups) oat flour

225g (1⅛ cups plus 2 tablespoons) buckwheat flour

1½ teaspoons baking soda

1 tablespoon baking powder

½ teaspoon cinnamon

2 teaspoons salt

100g (½ cup) light or dark muscovado sugar

1 tablespoon orange zest

1 teaspoon lemon zest

250g (1 cup plus 1 tablespoon) cold unsalted butter, cut into 1-cm (½-inch) cubes

300g (1¼ cups) crème fraîche

500g (18 ounces) grated apple (5 or 6 tart apples such as Discovery, Gravenstein, Cox's Orange Pippin, or Granny Smith)

1 egg beaten with 2 tablespoons milk, for the egg wash

Preheat the oven to 200°C/390°F (180°C/355°F convection). Line a baking sheet with parchment paper.

Combine all the dry ingredients in a mixing bowl along with the zests and whisk together well. Using a pastry cutter, the back of a fork, or a mixer, cut in the cubes of butter until they are the size of large peas.

Stir together the crème fraîche and grated apple. Mix this into the flour and butter mixture until it barely holds together. Turn out on to a flour-dusted surface and pat roughly into a square. Let the dough rest for 5 minutes, then flatten it to about 2.5cm (1 inch) thick with a rolling pin. Fold it in half so that you have a rectangle. Then fold it in half again into a small square. Let it rest for 7 minutes, then roll it into a square about 4cm (1½ inches) thick.

Use a sharp knife to cut the square into three long pieces. Cut each log into two and then each square into two triangles. Place on the lined baking sheet (or wrap in plastic wrap and store in the freezer), brush with the egg wash, and bake for about 35 minutes, or until golden brown.

These are best eaten on the day you bake them.

Sweet potato, coconut, date, and rye muffins

Sweet potatoes and dates impart a little warm sweetness to cakes, but mostly they give them great texture and moisture, which is important when baking with whole grain flours. Here I use a little agave syrup and no refined sugar.

Makes 12 large muffins

700g (1½ pounds; about 2 large) sweet potatoes, skins left on

300g (2 cups) whole grain rye flour

200g (1⅓ cups) whole grain spelt flour

½ teaspoon baking soda

1 tablespoon baking powder

1 teaspoon pumpkin pie spice

1 teaspoon kosher salt

4 eggs

1 teaspoon vanilla extract

300g (1¼ cups) unsweetened almond milk

200g (¾ cup plus 2 tablespoons) vegetable or coconut oil

150g (1½ cups) maple syrup

100g (¼ cup) agave syrup

150g (5 ounces; about 15 small) dates, pitted and cut into quarters

130g (1⅔ cups) shredded unsweetened coconut

50g (⅔ cup) coconut chips, for sprinkling on top

Preheat the oven to 180°C/355°F (160°C/320°F convection). Line a 12-cup deep muffin pan with paper liners and line a baking sheet with parchment paper.

Cut the sweet potatoes in half lengthwise and place, cut side down, on the lined baking sheet. Bake for about 25 to 30 minutes, or until tender. When they are cooked, scrape out the flesh and discard the skins. Roughly mash the sweet potatoes so that some of the mixture is smooth and some small chunks remain.

In a large bowl, combine the flours, baking soda, baking powder, pumpkin pie spice, and sea salt. Whisk these together and set aside.

In another bowl, whisk together the eggs, vanilla, almond milk, and oil. Stir in the maple and agave syrups, mashed sweet potato, quartered dates, and shredded coconut. Add this to the flour mixture and stir together until all the dry ingredients are just incorporated into the liquid. The batter will be thick. Allow the batter to sit for 10 minutes so that the flour can absorb some of the liquid.

Using an ice cream scoop or a large spoon, put two heaped scoops of batter into each liner. The liners will be very full, but this will result in that lovely domed muffin top when baked. Sprinkle with the coconut chips and bake for 35 to 40 minutes until the tops of the muffins are golden and springy to the touch.

Leave the muffins to rest for a few minutes before removing from the pan. Serve warm or at room temperature. These muffins are incredibly moist and will keep well for 3 days in an airtight container.

Bacon and egg buttermilk biscuits

Southern biscuits are everything I love about baking. They are easy and fast to make, so they deliver instant gratification; they are fluffy and buttery, so they comfort you; and they are often done badly, so a good biscuit is something to be really proud of. These biscuits are great filled with jams and compotes or bacon and eggs. It's important to bake them just before serving because they have zero shelf life, but you can make the dough ahead of time and pop the cut-out raw biscuits into the freezer until you want to bake them.

Makes 12 biscuits

700g (5 cups) all-purpose flour, plus more for rolling

2 tablespoons baking powder, plus 1½ teaspoons

1 tablespoon kosher salt

200g (¾ cup plus 2 tablespoons) cold unsalted butter, cut into 1-cm (½-inch) cubes

650g (2⅔ cups) buttermilk or plain yogurt

FOR THE FILLING

24 strips smoked bacon, cooked

12 eggs, boiled for 7 minutes
tomato ketchup or hot sauce, to taste

Preheat the oven to 220°C/430°F (200°C/390°F convection). Line a large baking sheet with parchment paper.

In a large bowl, whisk together the flour, all of the baking powder, and the salt. Using a pastry cutter, the back of a fork, or a mixer, cut the cubes of butter into the flour mixture until the butter is roughly the size of peppercorns. Stir in the buttermilk or yogurt until the dough comes together into a raggedy ball. It will be a bit wet and sticky, but this is what you are aiming for.

Transfer the dough to a lightly floured work surface and press or roll into a square about 3cm (1¼ inches) thick. Using a 7cm (2¾ inches) round cutter, stamp out 12 biscuits. Arrange the biscuits on the lined baking sheet so that they are almost touching each other, then pierce the biscuits with a fork. As they bake they will push each other up into fluffy biscuits.

Bake the biscuits for about 15 to 20 minutes, until the tops are golden and the biscuits are cooked through. When they come out of the oven, split them open and fill with crisp bacon and boiled eggs and ketchup or hot sauce, or your favorite condiment. These are best eaten on the day of baking.

Cinnamon buns

Of course a soft yeasty bun can be a wonderful thing, but at Violet we have never had enough space to work with yeasted bread doughs. They take up more room and need larger machines. I came up with these yeast-free buns in my home kitchen by looking back through the cookbooks of the 1950s, when everything was about how to make things more quickly. Quick breads, as breads leavened with baking powder or baking soda are called, were an alternative to time-consuming yeast or sourdough breads. Truly, they are something altogether different. They both have their place on the table. This recipe can also be made ahead and then frozen in the muffin tin until ready to bake.

Makes 12 buns

FOR THE FILLING

75g (⅓ cup) unsalted butter

250g (1 cup plus 2 tablespoons) light brown sugar

1 tablespoon ground cinnamon

FOR THE CINNAMON BUNS

560g (1½ cups) all-purpose flour, plus more for rolling

2 tablespoons baking powder

2 teaspoons kosher salt

2 teaspoons ground cardamom

240g (1 cup plus 1 tablespoon) cold unsalted butter, cut into small cubes

300g (1¼ cups) cold milk

sugar, for dipping

butter, for greasing the pan

Preheat the oven to 200°C/390°F (180°C/355°F convection).

Butter a 12-cup deep muffin pan.

First, prepare the filling. Melt the butter and leave in a warm place so that it remains liquid. Mix together the light brown sugar and cinnamon until no lumps remain, then set aside.

Now make the dough. In the bowl of a stand mixer with a paddle attachment, combine all the dry ingredients with the cubes of butter and mix until you have a coarse meal. Slowly pour in the cold milk while the mixer is running, until the dough forms into a ball and comes away from the bowl. Turn the dough out onto a lightly floured surface and leave to rest for a few minutes. Fold the dough gently over itself once or twice to pull it all together. Let the dough rest a second time, for 10 minutes.

Continued

Clear a large surface, dust lightly with more flour, and roll out the dough into a large rectangle until about 5mm (⅛ inch) thick. Brush the surface of the dough with the melted butter and, before the butter hardens, sprinkle the cinnamon sugar onto the butter. You want a good, slightly thick layer.

Now roll the dough up, starting at the long side, keeping it neat and tight. Gently tug the dough toward you to get a taut roll while rolling away from you into a spiral. Once it's all rolled up, gently squeeze the roll to ensure it's the same thickness throughout. Use a sharp knife to cut the roll crosswise into 12 even slices. Take a slice of the cinnamon roll, peel back about 5cm (2 inches) of the loose end of the pastry and fold it in back under the roll to loosely cover the bottom of the roll. Place in the muffin pan, flap side down. Repeat with the remaining slices.

Bake the buns for 25 minutes. As soon as they're out of the oven, flip them over onto a wire cooling rack so that they don't stick to the tray. Dip each cinnamon bun into a bowl of sugar and serve straight away.

Raspberry and star anise crumble muffins

Star anise is a spice that I usually associate with savory cooking. It appears in Chinese and Vietnamese foods, which I love, and is used to flavor meats and tea in India. But occasionally I like to add it to my sweet cooking. It is usually found whole, so you may need to grind it yourself. I have an old coffee grinder that I no longer use for coffee beans and instead have turned it into my spice grinder. If you still use yours for coffee, wipe it out and grind a hunk of bread in it. This cleans out the coffee flavor very well.

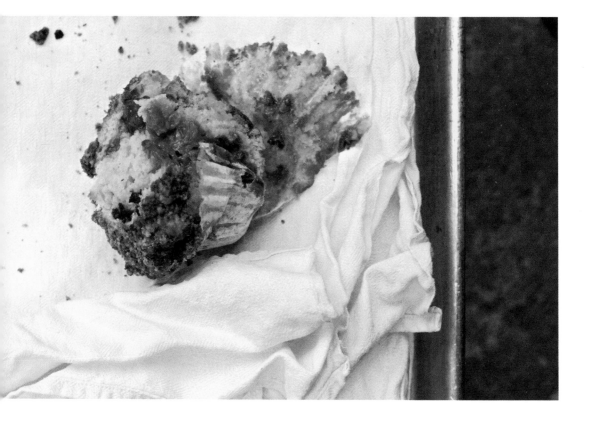

Makes 12 large muffins

FOR THE CRUMBLE TOPPING

125g (½ cup) cold unsalted butter

140g (1 cup) all-purpose flour

100g (1 cup plus 2 tablespoons)
  dark muscovado sugar

½ teaspoon ground star anise

½ teaspoon ground cinnamon

½ teaspoon ground ginger

¼ teaspoon kosher salt

FOR THE MUFFINS

200g (¾ cup plus 2 tablespoons)
  unsalted butter

600g (4¼ cups) all-purpose flour

4 teaspoons baking powder

½ teaspoon ground star anise

½ teaspoon ground cinnamon

½ teaspoon ground ginger

1 teaspoon kosher salt

3 eggs

250g (1¼ cups) sugar

2 teaspoons vanilla extract

300g (1¼ cups) whole milk

400g (2¾ cups) fresh or frozen
  (but if frozen, not defrosted)
  raspberries

Preheat the oven to 190°C/375°F (170°C/340°F convection). Line a deep
12-cup muffin pan with paper liners.

First make the crumble topping. Quickly mash all of the crumble ingredients
together and set aside while you make the muffins. The topping can be made
in advance and kept in the fridge for up to a week or in the freezer for up
to a month.

To make the muffins, melt the butter and set it aside to cool slightly but keep
it away from drafts.

In a large bowl, combine the flour, baking powder, spices, and salt and use
a whisk to mix it all together. Set aside.

In another bowl, whisk together the eggs and sugar until light and fluffy.
Gradually whisk in the melted butter, then the vanilla and the milk. Now add
this mixture to the dry ingredients along with the berries and gently stir
together just until the dry ingredients are incorporated, taking care not to
crush the berries. The batter will be thick.

If you have an ice cream scoop, use it to put two scoops of batter into each
paper liner. The liners will be very full, but this will give the muffins their
wonderful signature look when baked. Sprinkle the crumble topping over
the muffins and bake for 30 to 35 minutes, or until the tops of the muffins
are golden and springy to the touch.

Once the muffins are out of the oven, leave them to cool for about 10 minutes
before removing from the pan. They can be served warm or at room temperature
and are best eaten on the day you bake them.

Chocolate croissant bread pudding

Croissants are heavenly things when made properly. In my first ever baking job at age seventeen, I learned to make croissants at the Bovine Bakery in Point Reyes Station, California. For an entire summer I rose at 3:15 a.m. for a 4 a.m. start. Armando (the wonderful baker who trained me) and I would drink a vat of coffee and set to work sheeting the dough and carefully cutting the shapes; triangles for plain croissants and ham and cheese, rectangles for pain au chocolat and pain d'amande, and squares for apple turnovers. At Violet we lack the space for a pastry sheeter (a large machine that rolls the dough out for you in perfect sheets), so I decided not to make croissants when we first opened. A difficult decision, but the right one. You can't do everything. For a time we bought croissants in and, if any went unsold, they were transformed the next day into this luxurious pudding.

Serves 8

4 chocolate croissants
300g (1¼ cups) heavy cream
900g (3¾ cups) whole milk
a pinch of salt
1 vanilla pod, seeds scraped out

230g (1 cup plus 2 tablespoons) sugar
7 eggs
2 tablespoons cocoa powder
50g (⅓ cup) dark chocolate (70 percent cocoa solids), broken into bite-size pieces

Preheat the oven to 180°C/355°F (160°C/320°F convection) and butter a deep 20 by 30-cm (8 by 12-inch) baking dish. Find another baking dish that is large enough to hold your baking dish (you will be making a bain-marie later to gently cook the custard).

Tear the croissants into pieces and place loosely on a baking sheet. Toast in the oven for 10 minutes, turning the pieces halfway through, until crunchy.

Put the cream and milk into a large, heavy-bottomed pan. Add a pinch of salt and the seeds scraped from the vanilla pod along with the pod itself. Place over medium-low heat and just before the mixture starts to simmer, or when it starts to "shiver," remove from the heat.

Meanwhile, in a clean bowl, whisk your sugar and eggs into frothy ribbons.

When the milk is ready, pour a third of it into the sugar and egg mixture, whisking constantly. Add the remaining milk and whisk in the cocoa powder. Strain the mixture into a bowl or jug. Save the vanilla pod, rinsing it well under cool water and laying it out to dry before adding it to your homemade Vanilla Extract (page 228).

Put the toasted bread into your buttered baking dish, then pour the chocolate custard over it, so that the bread is covered in custard (you will have some custard left over), and let it soak for 30 minutes. Save the rest of the custard for later.

After 30 minutes, add the remaining custard and scatter the chocolate pieces on top. Place the baking dish inside the larger dish and place in the oven. At this point, use a jug to pour water into your bain-marie so that it comes at least halfway up the side of the dish. Check the custard after 30 minutes. Bake until just set.

Strawberry, ginger, and poppy seed scones

These pretty pink-and-white scones dotted with blue or black poppy seeds are, for me, a perfect weekend scone. Make them with sweet summer strawberries and sharp crystallized ginger. I made these years ago when I was house-sitting in San Francisco for my then-boss at the clothing boutique Metier. As I was leaving, I ate one but left the rest behind for the family to come home to. Sheri talked about these scones for years, always encouraging me to pursue baking professionally.

Makes 8 to 10 large scones

320g (2¼ cups) all-purpose flour, plus more for the work surface

50g (¼ cup) sugar

2 teaspoons baking powder

40g (4 tablespoons) poppy seeds

1 teaspoon lemon zest

170g (¾ cup) cold unsalted butter, cut into 1-cm (½-inch) cubes

250g (1 cup) crème fraîche or sour cream

150g (5 ounces) crystallized ginger, chopped

150g (1 cup) strawberries, chopped

1 egg beaten with a little milk or cream, for brushing on top

1 tablespoon demerara sugar

Line a large baking sheet with parchment paper.

In a large bowl, whisk together the flour, sugar, baking powder, seeds, and lemon zest.

Add the cubes of butter and mix together with a pastry cutter or the back of a fork. Work quickly to keep your ingredients as cold as possible. You can of course do this in a food processor or stand mixer, using the paddle attachment.

Now add the crème fraîche or sour cream, chopped ginger, and berries and mix quickly to combine. Do not overmix or knead the scone dough, but quickly toss the ingredients together. Allow the dough to rest for 5 minutes.

On a lightly floured surface, turn the dough out and pat it into a square about 3.5 to 4cm (1½ inches) thick. Let it rest for 5 minutes. Pat the dough down again to form a circle and use a 6 to 7cm (2½ inches) pastry cutter or the rim of a glass to make 8 scones. Place on the lined baking sheet, brush with the egg and cream mixture and sprinkle with the demerara sugar. Place in the fridge for 10 minutes to chill. Meanwhile, preheat your oven to 180°C/355°F (160°C/320°F convection).

When ready, bake the scones for 15 to 20 minutes until slightly golden. Once they are out of the oven, transfer to a wire rack to cool.

These are best eaten on the day you bake them.

Ham, cheese, and leek scones

I love leeks. I love garlic. I love onions. All alliums are sacred to me because they create so much beautiful flavor when used properly. Sure, they are capable of leaving you with a bit of smelly breath, but isn't it worth it? Besides, if you're eating them with your partner or a friend, neither of you will really notice. Leeks are my favorite, especially when slowly cooked down into a silky creamy consistency so they become sweet and nuanced.

Makes 12 large scones

2 leeks

25g (2 tablespoons) unsalted butter

2 tablespoons olive oil

1 teaspoon flaky sea salt
  (such as Maldon)

a good grind of black pepper

200g (½ cup) parmesan, grated

450g (3¼ cups) all-purpose flour,
  plus more for the work surface

2 tablespoons baking powder

100g (7 tablespoons) cold unsalted
  butter, cut into cubes

500g (2 cups) plain yogurt

200g (7 ounces) of your favorite
  ham (Parma, Serrano, Bayonne,
  or country), cut into
  bite-size pieces

1 teaspoon kosher salt

1 egg, lightly beaten with a little
  milk or water, for the egg wash

Trim the roots and the tough green stalks and outer layer from the leeks. Cut the leeks in half lengthwise and run under cool water to rinse, peeling back the layers to get inside where the grit is lodged. Slice the leeks crosswise into 4-mm (¹⁄₁₆-inch) slices and drop into a bowl of cold water for about 10 minutes. All the dirt will fall to the bottom. Scoop the leeks out (rather than pouring them out with the water) and place in a colander to drain. Pat dry.

In a heavy-bottomed frying pan over medium-low heat, heat the 25g (2 tablespoons) of butter and the oil until the butter starts to foam. Add the leeks, flaky sea salt, and black pepper and sauté for about 10 to 15 minutes until soft but without color. When they are cooked, tip them into a bowl and chill in the fridge for about 20 minutes (this can be done the day before).

Line a baking sheet (or other container that can fit into your fridge) with parchment paper.

In a medium bowl, stir together the parmesan, flour, and baking powder. Cut in the butter with a pastry cutter or the back of a fork (or use a mixer) until crumbly. Add the yogurt, ham, kosher salt, and cooled leeks. Mix quickly to combine and then pat into a cube and place on a lightly floured surface. Pat the dough into a thick log and cut out triangles from the log—you will have about 12. Place the scones on the lined baking sheet (or other container) and put in the fridge to chill until set, about 1 hour.

Preheat the oven to 180°C/355°F (160°C/320°F convection). Line a large baking sheet with parchment paper, place the chilled scones on it, and brush the scones with the egg wash.

Bake for 25 to 30 minutes until golden. Serve right away. You can also make the scones and freeze them, then bake as and when you need them. They keep well for a month in the freezer.

Yellow peach crumb bun

One of the first recipes I learned as a child was how to make the coffee cake
on the back of the Bisquick box. The buttery plain white cake topped with
perfectly brown-sugary crumble topping was dangerous stuff. I was basically
addicted and often made it after school when I was bored. A lot. One day
I didn't have enough mix in the box, so I had a look at the ingredients on the
back. It contained flour, baking soda, vegetable shortening, and powdered
buttermilk. Indeed, we had all of these ingredients at home and so I set
to work with the paradoxical task of recreating a packaged cake mix from
scratch. I now make a similar cake at Violet; we add fruit to it, which is
delicious. Yellow peaches with the skins left on are the prettiest. Sometimes
we add nuts to the crumble topping. And this is where your sense of taste

comes into play. Use whatever fruit is in season and then choose a nut to pair with it. For peach, I would use pecans or almonds. For apple or quince, I might use walnuts. This recipe makes a large cake, which is great for a brunch with friends. If you like, halve the recipe and bake in a 23-cm (9-inch) square pan.

Makes one 33 by 23-cm (13 by 9-inch) cake, which cuts into 12 to 16 buns

FOR THE CRUMBLE TOPPING

200g (1½ cups plus 2 tablespoons) all-purpose flour

1 tablespoon ground cinnamon

200g (1 cup plus 2 tablespoons) light brown sugar

150g (⅔ cup) cold unsalted butter, cut into 1-cm (½-inch) pieces

1 teaspoon kosher salt

80g (3 ounces) nuts (optional)

FOR THE BUN

200g (¾ cup plus 2 tablespoons) unsalted butter, plus more for greasing the pan

420g (3 cups) all-purpose flour

1 tablespoon baking powder, plus 1 teaspoon

½ teaspoon kosher salt

150g (¾ cup) sugar

3 eggs

1 tablespoon vanilla extract

300g (1¼ cups) plain natural yogurt

5 or 6 (about 650g/1½ pounds) yellow peaches (berries, apples, or plums work well too)

Preheat the oven to 190°C/375°F (170°C/340°F convection). Butter a 33 by 23 by 8-cm (13 by 9 by 2-inch) baking pan and line the bottom and sides with parchment paper.

First make the crumble. Put all the ingredients into a food processor and pulse until the size of large bread crumbs. Do not overmix or it will turn into a wet dough. Alternatively, you can mix it by hand with a pastry cutter or the back of a fork. Cover and place in the fridge until ready to use.

Now make the bun. In a small pan, melt the butter and leave to cool slightly. In a large bowl, whisk together the flour, baking powder, salt, and sugar.

In a separate bowl, whisk together the eggs, vanilla, and yogurt. Slowly drizzle the melted butter into the yogurt mixture, whisking constantly. Make a well in the dry ingredients and pour in the wet ingredients. Stir together gently until just combined. Pour into your prepared baking pan and set aside.

Slice the peaches into eighths or sixteenths, depending on their size, and scatter them randomly over the batter. Cover the fruit with the crumble mixture and bake for about 1 hour, until an inserted skewer comes out clean. Test for doneness. The crumb should be tender, not dry, but neither should it be wet. Allow to cool for 15 minutes before cutting into slices and serving.

Midday

The Violet Bakery Cookbook just wouldn't feel complete without including some of our quiches, bread puddings, and toasted cheese sandwiches. Over the years we have introduced many healthy savory options, but the ones that people come back for are these guilty pleasures. Melty cheese, flaky pastry, and gooey, custardy bread. Comfort food for rainy days, hangovers, and for special treats.

Quiches are made with a very flaky pastry, blind-baked until a deep golden brown. They are filled with seasonal vegetables and cheeses and sometimes a little ham. It was the space constraints of our kitchen that caused us to be mainly a vegetarian café and bakery, though we do source a beautiful cured Serrano ham from Spain that we add on occasion.

Savory bread pudding was thought up one day when we had overordered from our bread supplier. We use a French *levain* bread from Poilâne Bakery, which has an outpost in west London. I first heard about the legendary baker Lionel Poilâne when working at Chez Panisse. He tragically died in a helicopter crash; luckily, his daughter carries on the tradition and the family bread business is thriving. Monsieur Poilâne had been an inspiration to Steve Sullivan, who started baking bread at Chez Panisse before setting up the Acme Bread Company in Berkeley, California; and it was Poilâne who first brought these traditional country loaves to the attention of the urban elite. The city wanted the food of the rural countryside. This trend for simple and basic, flavorful fare is exactly the type of pure cooking that interests me. So we take his bread and we soak it in custard, then we layer it up with cheeses and vegetables, much like our quiche. It's a wonderful way to use up sourdough bread that is a bit too sour for a sweet preparation.

The toastie. Ahhh, the toastie. There is so much to be said about this simple sandwich. Bread, cheese, butter, and, occasionally, an allium, tomato, or a bit of ham. I have included our staple toasties here, but you could put just about anything between two pieces of bread and press it under a hot broiler or, failing that, between two frying pans, and presto . . .

Cheddar and green onion toastie with quince jelly

After quiche, this was our second savory offering at Violet. Neal's Yard Dairy in London, who supplies us with all our cheeses, sells us a wonderful mixture of grated Cheddars. They take the offcuts from the tasting room and the bits that are not suitable to sell because of their size, shape, or other imperfections, and grate them all up together. It is a smart product for them to sell as it avoids waste, but it is equally beneficial for us because it means we get a more intense mature Cheddar flavor than we could afford if we were to buy wheels of cheese. And the fact that it comes pregrated is a huge help to us, since we sell so many of these toasties each day. We serve this sandwich with a fruit jelly or preserve. My favorite is crab apple and blackberry, but red currant, quince, or gooseberry are all good options. The salty, savory sandwich, balanced with sweet and tart jelly, is what makes this toastie so satisfying.

sourdough bread
butter
mature Cheddar cheese, grated
green onions, thinly sliced
salt and pepper
garlic clove (optional)
fruit jelly or jam, to serve
cornichons, to serve (optional)

Slice the sourdough bread very thinly and spread one slice with a little butter. Add a scoop of grated Cheddar cheese and scatter with a few thin slices of green onion. Season with a little salt and pepper and top with a second slice of bread.

Heat a heavy-bottomed frying pan or a sandwich press. Melt a little butter inside it and add the sandwich. Resist the temptation to press too hard, or all the cheese will come out of the sides. If using a frying pan, flip, and toast until the bread is golden and the cheese is melted.

Transfer the toasted sandwich to a board and brush lightly with a clove of garlic. Serve on a plate with a little bowl of fruit jelly or jam on the side for dipping the sandwich into. This is also good with a few cornichons.

Lacinato kale, leek, and ricotta bread pudding

This savory bread pudding was inspired by one of my favorite pasta sauces.

Serves 12

900g (2 pounds; about 1 loaf)
   stale white sourdough bread,
   crusts removed and thinly sliced

butter, for greasing the pan

FOR THE BRAISE

2 large leeks

2 tablespoons olive oil

2 tablespoons chopped fresh
   summer savory or rosemary

400g (14 ounces) Lacinato or
   other kale

1 tablespoon good-quality olive oil

½ teaspoon chile flakes
   (I use the Turkish ones)

150g (5 ounces) Gruyère, grated

100g (¼ cup plus 2 tablespoons)
   ricotta cheese

salt and pepper, to taste

FOR THE CUSTARD

8 eggs

5 tablespoons all-purpose flour

500g (2 cups) heavy cream

360g (1½ cups) whole milk

salt and pepper, to taste

a grate of nutmeg

Butter a 20 by 30-cm (8 by 12-inch) baking pan.

First, prepare the leeks. Trim the roots and the tough green stalks and outer layer from the leeks and discard. Cut the leeks in half lengthwise and run under cool water to rinse, peeling back the layers to get inside where the grit is lodged. Slice the leeks crosswise into 4-mm (1/16-inch) slices and drop into a bowl of cold water for about 10 minutes. All the dirt will fall to the bottom. Scoop the leeks out (rather then pouring them out with the water) and place in a colander to drain. Pat dry.

In a heavy-bottomed frying pan over medium-low heat, heat the oil. Add the leeks, savory or rosemary, and salt and pepper to taste, and sauté for about 10 to 15 minutes until soft but without color.

Bring a large pot of water to a boil and add enough salt to make it taste of the sea. Usually I add about 2 to 3 teaspoonfuls to a large pot of water. Strip the leaves of the kale away from the tough inner core and discard the core. Coarsely chop the leaves into 2-cm (¾-inch) strips and drop into the boiling water for about 3 to 5 minutes, or until tender. Do this in batches if your pan is not large enough, then remove from the pan with a slotted spoon and place in a large bowl. Season with salt and pepper and toss with the tablespoon of olive oil, the chile flakes, and the sautéed leeks. Set aside.

Grate the Gruyère and weigh out the ricotta, then set these aside as well.

In a bowl, whisk together the custard ingredients and then strain through a fine sieve into a jug.

In your prepared baking pan, layer the bread, kale mixture, and half the Gruyère, then dot with the ricotta. Pour two-thirds of the custard over the cheese, then sprinkle with salt, pepper, and nutmeg. Let the pudding rest for at least 30 minutes to absorb the custard.

Meanwhile, preheat the oven to 180°C/355°F (160°C/320°F convection). Cover the pudding with the remaining Gruyère and pour the remaining custard over the top.

Bake for 1 hour, until golden. Cut into portions and serve warm or at room temperature.

Tomato and marjoram tarts

You can put any topping you like on these delicious tarts. The original inspiration for these was the French *pissaladière* anchovy and onion tart. There is something so perfect about caramelized onions and pastry. It just works. I have a window box full of marjoram, and when it flowers in midsummer, I sprinkle the flowers onto the tarts as well.

Makes 4 individual
or 1 whole tart

FLAKY PASTRY

140g (1 cup) all-purpose flour, plus
    more for rolling and sprinkling

a pinch of salt, plus more for sprinkling

a pinch of sugar

85g (6 tablespoons) cold butter,
    cut into 1-cm (½-inch) cubes

2 to 3 tablespoons ice water

olive oil, for sprinkling

1 egg, lightly beaten, for the egg wash

FOR THE FILLING

2 yellow onions

2 tablespoons good-quality olive oil

a little salt

6 to 8 medium tomatoes,
    cut into 1-cm (½-inch) slices

2 tablespoons picked marjoram leaves

2 good pinches of sea salt, or to taste

plenty of cracked black pepper

To make the pastry, combine the flour, salt, and sugar in a bowl. Cut in the cubes of butter with a pastry cutter or the back of a fork, or use a stand mixer. Avoid overmixing, as you want to leave larger chunks of butter than you would think, to give a flakier pastry. Drizzle in the water and bring it all together. Shape into a ball, wrap in plastic wrap, and rest in the fridge for 30 minutes.

Meanwhile, make the filling. Slice the onions thinly. Heat the oil in a heavy-bottomed frying pan and sauté the onions with a little salt over low heat until they are soft and translucent.

TASTE. Taste your onions and see how salty they are. Taste your tomatoes and see how acidic they are. You may want to add a little more salt or olive oil to balance the flavor.

Preheat your oven to 200°C/390°F (180°C/355°F convection). Line a baking sheet with parchment paper.

If making individual tarts, divide the pastry into four balls and roll out on a lightly floured surface until about 2mm (1⁄16 inch) thick. Carefully lift onto the lined baking sheet and sprinkle with a little flour (to keep the pastry crisp). Cover with the onions and sliced tomatoes, leaving a 2-cm (¾-inch) border. Sprinkle with half the marjoram. Fold the rim of pastry up over the filling and brush the pastry with the beaten egg.

Bake the tarts for 20 to 25 minutes until golden. Sprinkle with a little olive oil, salt, pepper, and the remaining marjoram. Serve immediately.

Mozzarella, rosemary, and new potato tarts

I learned about this wonderful way with mozzarella from Pizzeria Delfina in San Francisco. You make a sauce of sorts with the cheese and the liquid that it comes in. Add a little cream and seasoning and you have one of the most delicious bases for a pizza or tart.

Makes 4 individual tarts or 1 large tart

FLAKY PASTRY

140g (1 cup) all-purpose flour, plus more for rolling and sprinkling

a pinch of salt

a pinch of sugar

85g (6 tablespoons) cold butter, cut into 1-cm (½-inch) cubes

2 to 3 tablespoons ice water

1 egg, beaten, for the egg wash

FOR THE FILLING

1 large ball buffalo mozzarella and the liquid it comes in

2 tablespoons heavy cream

2 tablespoons olive oil

1 tablespoon chopped rosemary leaves

2 good pinches of sea salt, or to taste

plenty of cracked black pepper

8 new potatoes (about 200g/7 ounces) peeled, boiled and cut into 1-cm (½-inch) slices

olive oil, for drizzling

To make the pastry, combine the flour, salt, and sugar in a bowl. Cut in the cubes of butter with a pastry cutter or the back of a fork, or use a mixer. Avoid overmixing, as you want to leave larger chunks of butter than you would think, to give a flakier pastry. Drizzle in the water and bring it all together. Shape into a ball, wrap in plastic wrap, and rest in the fridge for 30 minutes.

Meanwhile, make the filling. Chop the mozzarella ball into 1-cm (½-inch) pieces and put them in a bowl with 4 tablespoons of the cheese liquid, the cream, olive oil, rosemary, and salt and pepper. Mix the ingredients together, taste for seasoning and set aside.

Preheat your oven to 200°C/390°F (180°C/355°F convection). Line a baking sheet with parchment paper.

For individual tarts, divide the pastry into four balls. Roll it out on a lightly floured surface until about 2mm (1/16 inch) thick. Carefully lift onto the lined baking sheet and sprinkle with a little flour (this helps to keep the pastry crisp). Cover the base or bases with the sliced potatoes, leaving a 2-cm (¾-inch) border. Fold the rim of pastry up over the filling and brush the pastry with the beaten egg. Now spoon the cheese mixture evenly over the tarts.

Bake the tarts for 20 to 25 minutes, until golden. Remove from the oven and drizzle the baked tarts with a little olive oil before serving.

TASTE. Be sure always to boil your potatoes in salted water. The potatoes will absorb the salt from the water and it will bring out their flavor.

Squash, brown butter, and sage quiche

Butternut squash and sage with brown butter is a classic combination, but any sweet autumn squash works here.

Makes 1 deep (22 by 6-cm/9 by 2-inch) or standard (25-cm/10-inch) quiche, which serves 4 to 6

FLAKY PASTRY

140g (1 cup) all-purpose flour, plus more for rolling

a pinch of salt

a pinch of sugar

85g (6 tablespoons) cold butter, cut into 1-cm (½-inch) cubes

2 to 3 tablespoons ice water

1 egg, lightly beaten

butter, for greasing the pan

FOR THE FILLING

2 tablespoons all-purpose flour

3 eggs

200g (¾ cup) heavy cream

115g (½ cup) whole milk

2 good pinches of sea salt, or to taste

plenty of cracked black pepper

½ (about 600g/1⅓ pounds) butternut squash

3 sprigs of thyme

1 head of garlic

2 tablespoons olive oil

30g (2 tablespoons) unsalted butter

10 sage leaves

To make the pastry, combine the flour, salt, and sugar in a bowl and cut in the cubes of butter with a pastry cutter or the back of a fork, or use a stand mixer. Avoid overmixing, as you want to leave larger chunks of butter than you would think, which will result in a flakier pastry. Drizzle in the water and bring it all together. Shape into a ball, then wrap in plastic wrap, and let it rest in the fridge for at least 30 minutes.

Meanwhile, make the filling. Whisk the flour into one of the eggs to make a paste. Add the remaining eggs one at a time, mixing until fully incorporated. Whisk in the cream and milk. Strain this mixture into a bowl to remove any lumps of flour. Season with the sea salt and plenty of cracked black pepper. This can now sit while you prebake the pastry, or it can be made a day ahead.

Preheat your oven to 200°C/390°F (180°C/355°F convection). Butter a deep 22-cm (9-inch) tart pan. On a lightly floured surface, roll out your chilled pastry and press it into your buttered pan. Line with parchment paper and fill it with dried beans or ceramic weights, then bake for 25 minutes. Remove the beans and paper and brush the pastry with the beaten egg. Return it to the oven and continue baking for 15 to 20 minutes, until golden.

Meanwhile, line a baking sheet with parchment paper. Peel and slice your butternut squash into 5-mm (¼-inch) pieces, then spread them out on the lined baking sheet and sprinkle with the thyme. Slice the head of garlic through its middle, revealing the cross section of cloves. Place on the sheet too, and sprinkle with olive oil, salt, and pepper. Bake for 35 to 40 minutes, until soft.

Turn the oven down to 180°C/355°F (160°C/320°F convection). Fill the baked pastry with the roasted squash slices and squeeze the roasted garlic out of its skin onto the squash. Pour the egg and cream mixture over the top. Place the quiche on the lined baking sheet.

In a small frying pan over medium heat, melt the butter until it starts to sizzle and foam. Just as the white milk solids that have settled to the bottom of the pan start to turn golden brown, drop in your sage leaves. Let them sizzle and curl up for a moment, then take the pan off the heat. Drizzle over the quiche.

Bake for about 50 to 60 minutes until souffléd and golden. Leave to rest for 15 minutes or serve at room temperature.

Chipotle and cheddar corn muffins

Chipotle chiles are jalapeños that have been smoked. They can be bought dried or canned or even as a paste. Their smoky and slightly bitter flavor is a wonderful foil for sweet corn. I like using fine cornmeal in baking because it gives muffins and cakes a satisfying crunch, but it is a slightly bitter flour. It lends itself well to being a base for lifting other flavors.

Makes 12 muffins

150g (1 cup) all-purpose flour

200g (1¾ cups) fine cornmeal

1 teaspoon baking powder

½ teaspoon baking soda

1 teaspoon chile powder

1½ teaspoons kosher salt

½ teaspoon freshly ground
black pepper

2 tablespoons muscovado sugar

285g (2 cups) sweet corn, frozen or
cut from fresh ears (about 2 ears)

350g (1½ cups) sour cream or
crème fraîche

2 eggs

120g (½ cup) good-quality olive oil

4 green onions, thinly sliced

FOR THE CHEESE FILLING

200g (7 ounces) mature Cheddar
cheese, cut into 5-mm (¼-inch) cubes

1 tablespoon finely chopped fresh
marjoram or oregano

1 tablespoon chipotle paste, or
1 reconstituted dried chipotle pepper
with stem removed and chopped fine

1 teaspoon tomato paste

1 tablespoon good-quality olive oil

Preheat the oven to 200°C/390°F (180°C/355°F convection). Line a 12-cup muffin pan with paper liners.

First make the muffin mix. In a large mixing bowl, combine the flour, cornmeal, baking powder, baking soda, chile powder, salt, and pepper. Whisk these dry ingredients together well and set aside.

In another bowl, combine the muscovado sugar, sweet corn, and sour cream or crème fraîche and add the eggs and olive oil. Whisk these ingredients together, then add the sliced green onions and the flour mixture. Fold the ingredients together until they are incorporated.

Now make the cheese filling. In another small bowl, combine the Cheddar cheese with all the other ingredients. The cubes of cheese should be coated in the spicy mixture.

TASTE. Taste your cheese mixture at this point and decide if it needs a little additional seasoning—salt and pepper, more chipotle if you like things with a bite, or a little more tomato paste to sweeten the bitterness of the smoked chile.

Scoop half the muffin mix into the paper liners. Then distribute half of the cheese mixture evenly between the muffins and top with the remaining muffin mix. Finally, sprinkle with the remaining cheese.

Bake the muffins for 30 to 40 minutes, until an inserted skewer comes out clean. Leave to cool for about 10 minutes before removing from the pan. These muffins are best eaten within a day of baking.

Sour cream, chive, and feta scones

Savory scones are great alongside soups and salads or if you need to eat on the go. We all have days where we just haven't got time to stop and eat lunch, so a savory bite that you can hold in your hand can be a welcome sight. The dough is crumbly and dry when you are shaping it, but as it bakes, the butter melts into the layers, making the scones flaky and rich.

Makes 12 scones

400g (2¾ cups plus 2 tablespoons) all-purpose flour, plus more for rolling

1 tablespoon sugar

2½ teaspoons baking powder

½ teaspoon baking soda

½ teaspoon salt

¼ teaspoon freshly ground black pepper, plus more for the garnish

180g (¾ cup plus 1 tablespoon) cold unsalted butter, cut into 1-cm (½-inch) cubes

1 egg

200g (¾ cup plus 1 tabelspoon) sour cream

30g (½ cup) fresh chives, chopped

200g (7 ounces) feta cheese, broken into pieces

1 egg or egg yolk beaten with a little water or milk, for the egg wash

Preheat the oven to 200°C/390°F (180°C/355°F convection). Line a large baking sheet with parchment paper.

In a medium bowl, combine the flour, sugar, baking powder, baking soda, salt, and black pepper. Cut in the butter with a pastry cutter or the back of a fork (or use a stand mixer) until you have a crumbly mixture. Add the egg, sour cream, and chives. Mix the ingredients together quickly, then add the feta pieces and mix again until just combined, then pat into a cube and place on a lightly floured surface.

Let the dough rest for 5 minutes, then flatten it to about 2.5cm (1 inch) thick with a rolling pin. Fold it in half as if you were closing a book so that you have a rectangle. Then fold it in half again so that you have a small square. Wrap the dough in plastic wrap and put in the fridge to rest for 10 minutes. When it's chilled, roll the dough into a square about 5cm (2 inches) thick. Use a sharp knife to cut the square into three long pieces. Cut each log into two and then each square into triangles. Freeze or bake right away.

Continued

Place the chilled scones on the lined baking sheet and brush with the egg wash. Bake for 25 to 30 minutes, until golden. These are best eaten on the same day they are made. You can also make the scones, freeze them individually, and then bake as and when you need them. They will keep well for a month in the freezer.

Comté and chutney toastie

Comté is a cow's milk hard cheese that comes from the Franche-Comté region of France, where some of my favorite wine also comes from. Damian and I hired a camper van one summer and drove through France with our dog, Shuggie. We arrived in the sleepy mountain town of Pupillin and had an inspired wine tasting at the home of Anne and Emmanuel Houillon, who took over Pierre Overnoy's wine estate and now make his wine. This is one of the most beautiful unfiltered, unfined wines. The wine is organically produced, and sulfites are never added. It tastes so special because much care is taken in choosing the grapes, and they are picked and used at exactly the right moment so they are in the best condition. I realized that this is the same approach I take when choosing fruit for my puddings and cakes. The condition of the fruit is of vital importance—one moldy berry would spoil the flavor.

Anne and Emmanuel do all the work themselves with the help of just one farmhand. When we left, they had already sold out of their wine, so we headed to the mythical cheese and wine shop called Essencia in nearby Poligny. The proprietor had four wheels of Comté in various vintages—young and creamy or more mature and savory. We bought pieces from two different wheels, a little bread, and a single bottle of Overnoy (all we were allotted of the much-sought-after wine).

sourdough bread
butter
Comté cheese, thinly sliced
fruit chutney (we make our own apple and red onion
  chutney at Violet, but you can also buy great ones)
salt and pepper
garlic clove (optional)

Slice the sourdough bread very thinly and spread with a little butter. Place thinly sliced Comté cheese on one slice and a spoonful of good fruit chutney on another slice. Season with a little salt and pepper and sandwich together.

Heat a heavy-bottomed frying pan or a sandwich press. Melt a little butter inside it and add the sandwich. Resist the temptation to press too hard, or all the cheese will come out of the sides. If using a frying pan, flip, and toast until the bread is golden and the cheese is melted.

Transfer the toasted sandwich to a board, brush it lightly with a clove of garlic, and serve on a plate.

Braised fennel, olive, and caper bread pudding

Savory bread puddings are a great way to use up day-old bread. We now have access to many artisan sourdough breads in London, and as a new generation of bakers open their own bakeries and experiment with naturally leavened breads, the trend is spreading beyond large cities to small communities all over.

This recipe requires a good strong bread and is traditionally made with a country loaf. In the 1930s, when Pierre Poilâne reintroduced this type of bread to Parisians, it was a revelation. Up till then the trend had been for baguettes, but his bread, which was made with stone-ground wheat, sea salt, sourdough starter, and water and then baked in a wood oven, soon gained popularity. His son Lionel more than quadrupled the size of the business from the 1970s (collaborating with artists like Salvador Dalí, who would order objects and sculptures made of bread) until 2002, when he died in a helicopter crash. Lionel's daughter Apollonia runs the business today. We use this bread at Violet for all our toasties, and when we have some left over, we make this bread pudding.

Serves 12

900g (2 pounds; about 1 loaf) stale white sourdough bread, crusts removed and thinly sliced

butter, for greasing the pan

FOR THE BRAISE

3 tablespoons olive oil

2 fennel bulbs, cut into 2-cm (¾-inch) wedges, or 6 baby fennel cut into pieces

salt and pepper, to taste

6 large garlic cloves, unpeeled

2 tablespoons lemon juice

2 tablespoons wine vinegar (red or white)

1 small tomato, diced

100g (½ cup) water

1 tablespoon capers, rinsed

10 black wrinkly olives, pitted and halved

3 sprigs of thyme

1 teaspoon sugar

zest of ½ lemon

¼ to ½ teaspoon Aleppo or Marash (Turkish) chile flakes, plus more for sprinkling

a drizzle of good-quality olive oil

150g (5 ounces) Gruyère, grated

100g (¼ cup plus 2 tablespoons) ricotta

FOR THE CUSTARD

8 eggs

5 tablespoons all-purpose flour

500g (2 cups) heavy cream

360g (1½ cups) whole milk

a grate of nutmeg

salt and pepper, to taste

Continued

Butter a 20 by 30-cm (8 by 12-inch) baking pan.

To prepare the fennel, heat some oil in a large, heavy-bottomed pan with a lid and brown the fennel on both sides (do this in batches if your pan is not large enough). Remove from the pan and season with salt and pepper.

Pour more oil into the pan and add the garlic cloves. Fry for about 5 minutes to brown them slightly. Add the lemon juice and vinegar and reduce the mixture to half its volume over medium heat. Add the diced tomato, half the water, the capers, olives, thyme, and sugar and a pinch of salt and pepper. Return the fennel to the pan along with the remaining water and cook for 12 minutes. Add the lemon zest, chile flakes, and a drizzle of good olive oil. Remove the garlic cloves and set aside. Grate your Gruyère and weigh out the ricotta, then set these aside as well.

In a bowl, whisk together the custard ingredients and then strain through a fine sieve into a jug.

In your prepared baking dish, layer the bread, braised fennel, and half the Gruyère, then dot with the ricotta. Pour two-thirds of the custard over the top, then sprinkle with salt, pepper, nutmeg, and chile flakes. Let the pudding rest for at least 30 minutes to absorb the custard.

Meanwhile, preheat the oven to 180°C/355°F (160°C/320°F convection).

When ready, cover the pudding with the remaining Gruyère and pour the rest of the custard over it. Bake for 1 hour, until set and golden. Cut into portions and serve warm.

Sweet corn and roasted cherry tomato quiche

Quiche is a wonderful thing. It should be wobbly, never overcooked. There should be ample fillings, whether meat or vegetables or cheese, but these should not overcrowd the custard. The pastry should be well baked and flaky, never doughy or soggy. Cheese is good, but not compulsory. Seasoning is what can take it from mediocre to exceptional. Get all of these elements just right, and quiche becomes the perfect meal. Serve with greens tossed in vinaigrette.

Makes 1 deep (22 by 6-cm/9 by 2-inch) or standard (25-cm/10-inch) quiche, which serves 4 to 6

FOR THE PASTRY

140g (1 cup) all-purpose flour, plus more for rolling

a pinch of salt

a pinch of sugar

85g (6 tablespoons) cold unsalted butter, cut into 1-cm (½-inch) cubes

2 to 3 tablespoons ice water

1 egg, lightly beaten

butter, for greasing the pan

FOR THE FILLING

2 tablespoons all-purpose flour

3 eggs

200g (¾ cup) cream

115g (½ cup) whole milk

2 good pinches of sea salt, or to taste

plenty of cracked black pepper

150g (5 ounces) cherry tomatoes, halved

1 tablespoon olive oil

a sprinkle of salt and pepper

2 sprigs of thyme

1 ear of corn, cut from the cob

90g (3 ounces) soft goat's milk cheese

1 tablespoon chopped fresh summer savory or thyme

To make the pastry, combine the flour, salt, and sugar in a bowl. Cut in the cubes of butter with a pastry cutter or the back of a fork, or use a stand mixer. Avoid overmixing, as you want to leave larger chunks of butter than you would think. This will make the pastry more flaky. Drizzle in the water and bring it all together. Shape into a ball and wrap in plastic wrap. Leave to rest in the fridge for at least 30 minutes.

Meanwhile, make the filling. Whisk the flour into one of the eggs to make a paste. Add the remaining eggs one at a time, mixing until fully incorporated. Whisk in the cream and milk. Strain this mixture into a jug or bowl to remove any lumps of flour. Season with the salt and plenty of cracked black pepper. This can sit while you prebake the pastry, or it can be made a day ahead.

Preheat your oven to 200°C/390°F (180°C/355°F convection). Butter a tart pan—I use a deep tart pan that is about 22cm (9 inches) wide, but you could choose a wider, shallower pan. On a lightly floured surface, roll out your chilled pastry and press it into your buttered pan. Line the pastry with a sheet of parchment paper, then fill it with dried beans or ceramic weights and blind-bake for 25 minutes. Remove the beans and paper and brush the pastry with the lightly beaten egg. Return the pastry to the oven and continue baking for 15 to 20 minutes until golden.

Meanwhile, roast your halved cherry tomatoes with a drizzle of olive oil, a sprinkle of salt and pepper, and the sprigs of thyme. They will take about 30 minutes to dry out a bit and become more concentrated in flavor.

Turn the oven down to 180°C/355°F (160°C/320°F convection). Fill the baked pastry with the corn kernels and tomatoes, crumble in the goat's cheese, and sprinkle with the chopped summer savory or thyme. Pour the egg and cream mixture over the top. Place the tart pan on a baking sheet in the oven and bake for about 50 to 60 minutes until souffléd and golden. Leave in the pan for 15 minutes before turning it out. Quiche is also delicious at room temperature.

Afternoon

The best part about moving to London was discovering the third meal of the day. Teatime. Tea is the third of four meals a day in the UK, and it is awesome. You have breakfast around eight in the morning, and lunch around one or one-thirty. Then when you are starting to feel hungry but know that your dinner won't be until eight or eight-thirty in the evening, there is teatime. I generally like to take tea around four-thirty or five. Anything after five can spoil your appetite for dinner. As I don't like eating cake after dinner, the perfect time of day for me to have it is at teatime. I am not talking about the grand, hotel-style afternoon tea—though I do love this British tradition on a special occasion. I am talking about a simple cup of tea and slice of cake in the afternoon to get you through the day and reenergize you.

The best cakes to have at this time of day are less sweet ones, usually with little or no icing. Loaf cakes are a firm favorite. In America we sometimes refer to these cakes as quick breads because they are leavened with baking soda or baking powder rather than yeast. Think banana bread, ginger bread, and soda bread. Baking soda biscuits or scones are also the perfect afternoon treat. Spread with a good jam and filled with freshly whipped or clotted cream, they are just so good, especially on a cold rainy day when you are warm and cozy inside.

Cookies and bars are relatively quick to throw together. One of the simplest pleasures in life is a freshly baked, warm chocolate chip cookie. Whether you take yours with a glass of milk (or almond milk) or a cup of tea or coffee, there is no denying the immediate comfort that the taste of melted chocolate suspended in a warm, salty, gooey, brown-sugary dough brings. As a youngster, I would make a batch of cookie dough and then bake just two at a time in the toaster oven (like a mini convection oven) as an after-school snack. Now I keep already-portioned scoops of dough in my freezer and bake them off as and when I fancy one.

Banana buttermilk bread

For the first five years of Violet, I resisted adding banana bread to the menu. It always seemed to me like something you only made at home, with old bananas. I am not a huge fan of banana and, indeed, was never a huge fan of cake made from them. Eventually, however, I grew tired of telling customers we didn't have it and set out to make a version I could be proud of. This cake is now one of the most popular items on our menu, and for good reason.

Makes one (25 by 10-cm/10 by 4-inch) loaf cake, which cuts into 8 slices

butter, for greasing the pan

6 very ripe bananas

150g (⅔ cup) vegetable oil

200g (1 cup plus 2 tablespoons) dark brown sugar

1 teaspoon vanilla extract

1 teaspoon dark rum

2 eggs

75g (⅓ cup) cultured buttermilk or plain yogurt

210g (1½ cups) all-purpose flour

1 teaspoon baking soda

1 teaspoon baking powder

¼ teaspoon kosher salt

3 tablespoons sugar

Preheat the oven to 180°C/355°F (160°C/320°F convection). Butter a 25 by 10-cm (10 by 4-inch) loaf pan and line with parchment paper.

Reserve half a banana for the top of the cake and mash the remaining bananas well.

In a bowl, whisk together the oil, brown sugar, vanilla, rum, eggs, and buttermilk or yogurt. Add the mashed banana and set aside.

In another bowl, whisk together the flour, baking soda, baking powder, and salt. Fold this into the banana mixture until just combined, then pour into your prepared pan. Smooth the top with an icing spatula or rubber spatula and place the reserved banana half, cut lengthwise, on top. Sprinkle with the sugar.

Bake for 40 to 50 minutes, until an inserted skewer comes out clean and the top of the cake has set and starts to caramelize. I sometimes use a kitchen blowtorch to help this along. Leave to cool in the pan for about 10 minutes, then transfer to a wire rack to cool completely.

Coffee cardamom walnut cakes

I love the English coffee walnut cake that appears on the menu of every museum café and National Trust house I visit. I've always loved the flavor of coffee in cakes and desserts. When I was little, my favorite ice cream flavor was coffee and I could never say no to a coffee éclair. Adding cardamom to the sponge gives this walnut cake another depth. The three flavors marry very well.

Makes 12 individual cakes

butter, for greasing the pans

FOR THE SPONGE
75g (2½ ounces) walnuts
210g (1½ cups) all-purpose flour
¾ teaspoon baking powder
¾ teaspoon baking soda
½ teaspoon kosher salt
¾ teaspoon ground cinnamon
⅛ teaspoon ground cloves
1 teaspoon ground cardamom

1 teaspoon ground pink peppercorns
180g (¾ cup plus 1 tablespoon) unsalted butter, softened
150g (¾ cup) sugar
2 eggs
1½ teaspoons vanilla extract
210g (¾ cup plus 2 tablespoons) crème fraîche

FOR THE ICING
200g (1½ cups) confectioners' sugar
2 tablespoons freshly brewed strong coffee or espresso

Preheat the oven to 170°C/340°F (150°C/300°F convection). Brush a 12-cup muffin pan with melted butter.

First, warm the walnuts through on a baking sheet in the oven. Do not toast them; you just want to bring out the fragrant oils. This should take less than 5 minutes. Let the nuts cool slightly, then chop fine. Set aside.

In a large bowl, sift together the flour, baking powder, baking soda, salt, and spices, then whisk this mixture through the chopped nuts. Set aside.

In a stand mixer, whisk the butter and sugar until light and fluffy.

Add the eggs one at a time, mixing until each one is fully incorporated, then add the vanilla extract. Mix in the flour and nut mixture and then the crème fraîche.

Divide the batter among the 12 wells and bake for 20 minutes until the cakes spring back to the touch. Let the cakes cool in the pan for about 10 minutes, then gently pop them out (you may need to run a small paring knife around the insides of the wells to ease the cakes out). Place the cooled cakes upside down on a wire rack.

Whisk together the ingredients for the icing and spoon it over the cakes. Use the back of a spoon to gently guide it to the edges so that it willingly drips down the sides.

Buckwheat butter cookies

These cookies are super moreish. Buttery and crisp, they work well with creamy desserts, or they can be enjoyed with a cup of tea or coffee in the afternoon. Because they are made with buckwheat flour, they are gluten free. Buckwheat has long been a common ingredient in eastern European cuisine, but with the growing demand for gluten-free products, buckwheat flour is increasingly used in baking today. Its strong, nutty flavor means it's not suitable for every dish. It goes well with citrus flavors and vanilla but can struggle against other robust flavors like banana or chocolate. It is wonderful in nutty recipes.

Makes about 18 cookies

75g (2½ ounces) whole almonds with skins on, toasted and coarsely chopped

75g (½ cup) buckwheat flour

100g (7 tablespoons) unsalted butter, chilled and cut into 1-cm (½-inch) cubes

50g (¼ cup) palm or coconut sugar

¼ teaspoon salt

25g (1 ounce) candied grapefruit or citron peel, chopped

1 medium egg yolk

In a mixing bowl, combine the chopped almonds, flour, and butter. Mix into a coarse meal. Add the sugar, salt, and grapefruit peel and mix well. Add the egg yolk and mix just until the dough starts to come together.

Lay two large squares of parchment paper on your work surface. Divide the dough into two pieces and form each piece into a log shape about 5cm (2 inches) wide and 15cm (6 inches) long. Put each log on a sheet of parchment paper and then, working with one log at a time, roll up the paper, encasing the log, and twist the ends to seal the parcel. (See the Chocolate Sandwich Cookies pictures on page 146.) Transfer to two small trays and leave to rest in the fridge for about 1 hour.

When ready to bake, heat the oven to 170°C/340°F (150°C/300°F convection). Line two baking sheets with parchment paper.

Remove the parchment from the cookie logs and cut each log into 5-mm (¼-inch) slices. Place the slices about 3cm (1 inch) apart on the lined baking sheets.

Bake for 10 to 14 minutes until the cookies start to turn golden. These keep well for up to 1 week in an airtight container.

Apricot kernel upside-down cake

Upside-down cakes are great to make because you really get to play with the ratios of cake and fruit without worrying about the structure. This type of cake also lends itself to lots of variation in seasonal fruits, as many fruit combinations work with this simple sponge. If you're not familiar with apricot kernels, now's the time to get acquainted. The flavor of the kernel, also known as a *noyau*, is similar to bitter almond, which is used to make almond extract. Apricot kernels are used in the making of Amaretto Disaronno liqueur. This cake is delicious served with cream and even more so if you add a splash of Disaronno.

Makes one 23-cm (9-inch) cake, which serves 8 to 10

FOR THE FRUIT TOPPING

300g (10½ ounces) apricots

200g (7 ounces) raspberries

75g (6 tablespoons) sugar

4 apricot kernels, crushed

½ vanilla pod, seeds scraped out

FOR THE SPONGE

150g (⅔ cup) butter, softened, plus more for greasing the pan

150g (¾ cup) sugar

2 eggs

½ teaspoon salt

200g (1¼ cups plus 2 tablespoons) all-purpose flour

1 teaspoon baking powder

whipping cream or crème fraîche, to serve

a little Amaretto Disaronno, to serve (optional)

Preheat the oven to 180°C/355°F (160°C/320°F convection). Butter a 23-cm (9-inch) layer pan and line with parchment paper. If it has a loose bottom, wrap the outside tightly with foil.

First, prepare the fruit topping. Cut the apricots into quarters and toss in a bowl with the raspberries, the 75g (6 tablespoons) of sugar, the crushed apricot kernels, and the vanilla seeds. (Don't discard the pod. Use it to make Vanilla Extract—see page 228.) Arrange the fruit in the bottom of the cake pan and set aside.

For the sponge, whisk the butter and sugar together in a stand mixer until light and fluffy and pale in color (or mix by hand if you don't have a mixer, but make sure the butter is very soft). Add the eggs one at a time, mixing well until each one is fully incorporated, then add the salt.

Continued

In another bowl, whisk together the flour and baking powder, then mix this into the butter mixture until just incorporated. Spread this over the fruit and smooth the top with an icing spatula or rubber spatula.

Bake for 30 minutes, until an inserted skewer comes out clean. The fruit will start to bubble up and the top of the cake will be golden and springy.

Allow the cake to cool in the pan for 20 minutes. To serve, run a paring knife along the inside of the pan and turn the cake out, apricot-side up, onto a suitable serving plate. Serve with crème fraîche or whipping cream flavored with a little Disaronno if you want.

Lemon drizzle loaf

All our lemons at Violet come from the Amalfi coast of Italy. They are large and sweet and have a very thick and pithy peel.

Makes one (25 by 10-cm/10 by 4-inch) loaf cake, which cuts into 8 slices

FOR THE SPONGE

265g (1 cup plus 3 tablespoons) unsalted butter, softened, plus more for greasing the pan

265g (1⅓ cups) sugar

zest of 3 or 4 lemons (save the juice for the lemon drizzle and icing)

3 eggs

265g (1¾ cups plus 2 tablespoons) all-purpose flour

1½ teaspoons baking powder

¼ teaspoon salt

100g (6½ tablespoons) milk

FOR THE LEMON DRIZZLE

1 tablespoon sugar

1 tablespoon water

2 tablespoons fresh lemon juice

FOR THE ICING

250g (1¾ cups) confectioners' sugar

2 tablespoons lemon juice

Preheat your oven to 180°C/355°F (160°C/320°F convection). Butter a 25 by 10-cm (10 by 4-inch) loaf pan and line the base and sides with parchment paper, extending the paper about 5cm (2 inches) above the top of the pan.

First make the sponge. In the bowl of a stand mixer, cream the butter and sugar well, though you don't want as fluffy a mixture as you would for a layer cake. Zest the lemons into the butter mixture and mix thoroughly. Beat in the eggs one at a time, making sure each one is thoroughly mixed in before adding the next.

In a large bowl, whisk together the flour, baking powder, and salt. Mix half of this into the creamed butter mixture, scraping down the sides, until barely combined.

While the mixer is still going, beat in all the milk. Then add the remaining flour and mix until just combined. Scrape the bowl and give it one last mix.

Scoop the mixture into the prepared pan and smooth the top with an icing spatula or rubber spatula.

Bake for 50 to 60 minutes, until the top of the cake is springy and an inserted skewer comes out clean.

To make the lemon drizzle, combine the sugar, water, and lemon juice in a small pan and heat just until the sugar is melted. Do not let this boil, or the fresh flavor will be lost.

Use a skewer to poke holes evenly throughout the baked loaf. Pour the lemon drizzle over the loaf and let it soak in while you make the icing.

In a small bowl, whisk together the confectioners' sugar and lemon juice until smooth.

To remove the loaf cake from the pan, run a small paring knife along the inside of the pan, then tilt the pan on its side and coax the loaf out, using the parchment paper as a handle. Peel off the paper and turn the loaf upright on your cooling rack or worktop. Drizzle the icing over the loaf and let it drip down the sides. Use a spatula to lift the loaf onto a serving dish. This keeps well for up to 3 days in an airtight container.

Nutty chocolate Barbados biscuits

These cookies are an almond macaroon of sorts, being primarily made up of egg whites and nuts, and they are naturally gluten free. I called them Barbados biscuits, because of the origin of the brown sugar that I used the first time I made them, and because of the alliteration. Another cool thing about these little cookies is that the sliced pecans look like little Batman wings.

Makes about 36 cookies

100g (3½ ounces) dark chocolate (70 percent cocoa solids)

125g (1 cup plus 1 tablespoon) ground almonds

125g (4½ ounces) pecans, chopped coarsely, plus 50g (1½ ounces) pecans sliced crosswise for the topping

150g (¾ cup plus 2 tablespoons) dark brown sugar

1 tablespoon cocoa powder

2 egg whites

1½ teaspoons vanilla extract

Preheat the oven to 180°C/355°F (160°C/320°F convection). Line a large baking sheet (or two small baking sheets) with parchment paper.

In a heatproof bowl, melt the chocolate over a pan of barely simmering water, stirring occasionally as it melts. (Do not let the bottom of the bowl touch the water.) Leave to cool slightly.

Put the nuts, sugar, and cocoa into a food processor and process until fine. Add the melted chocolate, the egg whites, and the vanilla and mix well.

Using an ice cream scoop or two dessert spoons, scoop individual portions of cookie dough onto the lined baking sheet, leaving enough space between each one to allow them to spread. Flatten them slightly with the underside of a glass or a measuring cup, then top each cookie with a slice of pecan.

Bake for 15 to 20 minutes or until the biscuits have set and puffed up but are still chewy on the inside. These keep well for up to 1 week in an airtight container.

Red plum Victoria sponge

The traditional recipe for Victoria sponge cake uses equal measures of eggs, butter, sugar, and flour, which results in a rich and slightly dense sponge. While I quite like the traditional sponge, I prefer a slightly lighter version containing milk, and this is the same sponge we use for vanilla cakes and cupcakes. It is a very versatile American yellow cake (the "yellow" refers to the egg yolks in the cake batter). The key to baking this cake is to keep the temperature low and cook it slowly. You are aiming for as flat a cake as possible, although a slightly rounded top looks nice too. I like to use a tart jam, such as our plum jam, in this cake, but you could use any good jam.

Makes one 20-cm (8-inch) cake,
which serves 8 to 10

125g (½ cup) unsalted butter, softened,
  plus more for greasing the pan

200g (1 cup) sugar

3 eggs

1 teaspoon vanilla extract

½ teaspoon salt

300g (2 cups plus 2 tablespoons)
  all-purpose flour

2 teaspoons baking powder

160g (⅔ cup) whole milk

700g (3 cups) whipping cream

plum jam (see recipe on page 254),
  at room temperature

confectioners' sugar, for dusting

Preheat the oven to 150°C/300°F (130°C/265°F convection). Butter a deep
20 by 7.5-cm (8 by 3-inch) cake pan and line with parchment paper.

In the bowl of a stand mixer, cream the very soft butter with the sugar
until almost white and fluffy. Gradually add the eggs, vanilla, and salt
and mix until fully incorporated.

In a separate bowl, whisk together the flour and baking powder, then add
half of it to the butter mixture until just combined. Add the milk and mix
until combined.

Now mix in the remaining flour. Scrape the bottom of the bowl and mix
once more. Pour the batter into your prepared pan and smooth the top
with an icing spatula or rubber spatula.

Bake for about 50 to 60 minutes, until the top of the cake springs back
to the touch. Allow the cake to cool for 15 to 20 minutes, then remove
it from the pan and set on a wire rack to cool completely.

Meanwhile, whip your cream to soft peaks and bring your jam to room
temperature if it is kept in the fridge.

Once the cake has cooled, use a long serrated knife to slice horizontally
through the center of the cake. Use the loose bottom of a springform pan
to slide in between the layers and lift off the top layer. Slide the bottom
layer off the cooling rack and onto a serving plate or cake stand. Spread
the bottom layer with a generous amount of jam and then dollop large
spoonfuls of whipped cream on top. Smooth the cream a little, then add
the top layer of sponge. Dust with confectioners' sugar and serve.

Oatmeal and candied peel cookies

At Violet we make our own candied citrus peel. I highly recommend you get into the habit of making your own, as the stuff you buy in the shops can be bland and waxy, which sort of defeats the purpose. Candied peel takes a few days to make, but it keeps in the fridge for up to a year. It's such a lovely thing to make with the leftover peel from your morning's juicing.

Makes 16 large cookies

250g (1 cup plus 1 tablespoon) unsalted butter, softened

200g (1 cup plus 2 tablespoons) light brown sugar

100g (½ cup) sugar

1 egg

1½ teaspoons vanilla extract

210g (1½ cups) all-purpose flour

1 teaspoon baking soda

1 teaspoon cinnamon

1 teaspoon kosher salt

150g (1½) cups rolled oats

100g (a generous ½ cup) golden raisins

50g (1¾ ounces) candied citrus peel, chopped

Line a small baking sheet or baking pan (one that will fit inside your freezer) with parchment paper.

In the bowl of a stand mixer, cream the butter and sugars until well combined but not light and fluffy. Add the egg and vanilla and mix well.

In another bowl, whisk together the flour, baking soda, cinnamon, sea salt, and rolled oats. Add this to the creamed butter mixture along with the raisins and citrus peel, and mix to combine.

Using an ice cream scoop or two dessert spoons, scoop individual portions of cookie dough onto the lined baking sheet. If using spoons, pat each portion into a little ball. Cover with plastic wrap and freeze for at least 1 hour, or up to a month. If you want, you can bake them right away, but the cookies will be slightly flatter and less even than the ones shown here.

When ready to bake, preheat your oven to 180°C/355°F (160°C/320°F convection). Line a large baking sheet with parchment paper and arrange the cookies evenly on it, leaving enough space between each one so they have room to expand during baking (they will almost double in size). If you are baking from frozen, allow the cookies 5 to 10 minutes out of the freezer before placing in the oven.

Bake for 18 minutes, until the center of each cookie is slightly soft and underbaked but the edges are crispy and golden. Remove from the oven and allow to cool on the tray for 10 minutes before serving. These cookies will keep up to 5 days in an airtight container.

Chocolate oat agave cookies

These cookies are deeply satisfying. Oaty and chocolatey in equal measure, they are sweetened only with agave nectar. There is, of course, a small amount of sugar in the chocolate itself, so you could replace the chocolate with cacao nibs or use chocolate made with 100 percent cocoa solids. We used to call this "the vegan cookie," but found that nonvegans wanted to try it, too. It is made with gluten-free oats and other gluten-free flours. We substitute flaxseed for the eggs, because the flax meal thickens the dough and binds it together in the same way eggs do, and instead of butter and milk, we use vegetable oil and shredded apples. Once we changed the name, these cookies remained popular with our loyal vegan and sugar-free customers, but new fans caught on too. If you can't find oat flour, pulverize rolled oats in a food processor.

Makes 12 large cookies

190g (1¾ cups) oat flour

50g (6 tablespoons) chickpea flour

30g (3 tablespoons plus 1½ teaspoons) arrowroot flour

3 tablespoons plus 1 teaspoon potato flour

1 teaspoon xanthan gum

¾ teaspoon baking soda

¾ teaspoon kosher salt

30g (¼ cup) ground flaxseeds

100g (¼ cup plus 1 tablespoon) agave nectar

150g (⅔ cup) vegetable oil

75g (2½ ounces) apple, peeled, cored, and processed in a food processor

1½ tablespoons vanilla extract

150g (5 ounces) dark chocolate (70 percent cocoa solids), broken into small pieces

Preheat the oven to 180°C/355°F (160°C/320°F convection). Line a large baking sheet with parchment paper.

In a large bowl, whisk together all the dry ingredients, mixing them well.

In another bowl, whisk together the agave nectar, vegetable oil, apple, and vanilla, then pour into the dry ingredients and stir in the chocolate pieces to combine.

Using an ice cream scoop or a couple of dessert spoons, scoop portions of the cookie dough onto the lined baking sheet, then use the underside of a glass or a measuring cup to press them into 1-cm (½-inch) thick disks.

Bake for about 15 minutes, until the cookies are a light golden color, crisp on the outside and still slightly soft on the inside.

These cookies keep very well in an airtight container for up to a week. The unbaked cookies also freeze well.

Ginger molasses cake

The Violet ginger cake is made with freshly grated ginger, cloves, earthy molasses, and cinnamon. I love the taste of cloves but only when you can barely detect it, as a subtle supporting act. This cake is simple, but the order of things is crucial for it to turn out correctly.

Makes one 23-cm (9-inch) cake or two 15-cm (6-inch) cakes, serving 8 to 10

FOR THE SPONGE

150g (5 ounces) fresh ginger

300g (2 cups plus 2 tablespoons) all-purpose flour

¾ teaspoon ground cinnamon

¼ teaspoon ground cloves

150g (¾ cup) sugar

200g (¾ cup plus 2 tablespoons) vegetable oil

250g (¾ cup) molasses

225g (1 cup) boiling water

2 teaspoons baking soda

2 eggs

butter, for greasing the pan

FOR THE LEMON GLAZE

250g (1¾ cups) confectioners' sugar

2 to 3 teaspoons fresh lemon juice

Preheat the oven to 150°C/300°F (130°C/265°F convection). Butter a 23-cm (9-inch) cake pan (or two 15-cm/6-inch layer pans) and line with parchment paper.

Peel the ginger and cut into 2-mm (1/16-inch) slices. Pulverize the ginger in a food processor and set aside.

In a bowl, combine the flour, cinnamon, and cloves. Whisk and set aside.

In a separate bowl, combine the sugar, oil, and molasses and whisk well.

Pour the boiling water into a glass jug and stir in the baking soda. Pour this into the sugar mixture and whisk well (the mixture should start to get foamy on top). Add the ginger and mix until evenly combined. Add the flour mixture, making sure you mix in the same direction (e.g., clockwise) the entire time. Don't change direction or you will get flour lumps. Don't overmix or the cake will be tough and dense.

Whisk the eggs in a separate, clean bowl and add to the cake batter until just combined. Pour into your prepared cake pan (or pans) and bake for about 1 hour, until an inserted skewer comes out clean and the top of the cake springs back to the touch. Leave to cool in the pan for about 10 minutes, then turn out onto a wire rack to cool completely.

Whisk together the confectioners' sugar and lemon juice until smooth and drizzle over the top. This cake keeps well for up to 5 days in an airtight container.

Honey and rose water madeleines

Antique madeleine molds were one of the first things I hung up on the wall at Violet when I opened the shop. These beautiful hand-forged molds came to me through a friendly customer in the early days of my stall on Broadway Market. He visited the stall each week with his wife and young daughter to buy cakes and have a chat, then one week he came armed with these wonderful antique molds. I bought two of the four or five he had, and now I kick myself for not buying the lot. I adore madeleines, and always have. My mom introduced them to me as a girl. I love the delicate seashell shape and the fact that they are like a mini cake more than a cookie. They are best eaten straight after baking.

NOTE. You will need a 12-cup madeleine mold to make these.

Makes 12 madeleines

100g (7 tablespoons) unsalted butter, melted, plus more for greasing the mold

1 tablespoon honey

2 teaspoons rose water

100g (½ cup) sugar

2 medium eggs

100g (¾ cup) all-purpose flour, plus more for dusting the mold

¾ teaspoon baking powder

FOR THE ICING

2 to 3 tablespoons rose syrup (I use Rose Brand Delicious Syrup from T.G. Kiat in Singapore, but you could use rose water and a little pink coloring or just leave out the coloring.)

200g (¾ cup) confectioners' sugar

First, prepare your madeleine mold. Melt a good amount of butter and leave to cool slightly, then brush it in the mold and dust with flour. Place the mold in your freezer for 5 to 10 minutes, then repeat the process. This trick really works! (If you are using a silicone madeleine mold, you can omit this second step.) Keep the mold in the freezer until you are ready to use it.

Preheat the oven to 160°C/320°F (140°C/285°F convection).

In a heatproof bowl set over a pan of barely simmering water, carefully melt the butter, then remove it from the heat and leave to cool slightly. Add the honey to the butter to dissolve it, then add the rose water.

In a bowl, whisk together the sugar and eggs until smooth. Whisk in the melted butter and honey mixture.

In another bowl, whisk together the flour and baking powder. Whisk this mixture into the egg and butter mixture until smooth. Spoon the batter into the prepared mold.

Bake for 10 to 12 minutes, until the madeleines have formed a peak in their middles and the tops spring back to the touch. Remove them from the oven and leave to cool in the mold for a minute or two while you make the icing.

Whisk the rose syrup into the confectioners' sugar until it is runny.

Turn the madeleines out of the mold and dip them in the icing. Serve right away—they are best eaten within the hour. (You can make the madeleine mixture in advance and bake it just before you want to serve these.)

Cream scones

At Violet the scones come out of the oven around two in the afternoon. Much as I would love to make more cakes with fresh cream, we don't have the capacity for this in the shop or in our fridges. But since we love the thick, rich cream that we get from Somerset, and because we make so many delicious quick jams for filling cakes and serving with toast, we simply had to make some scones to go with them. My scones are a bit like an American shortcake—that is to say they are made with a lot of butter and no eggs. To make them extra-rich we put cream in the dough. Everything, once assembled, becomes better than the sum of its parts. I think these scones work best with a tart berry or currant jam.

Makes 12 scones

700g (5 cups) all-purpose flour,
  plus more for rolling

2 tablespoons baking powder

100g (½ cup) sugar

½ teaspoon salt

200g (¾ cup plus 2 tablespoons)
  unsalted butter, chilled

600g (2½ cups) heavy cream

1 egg, lightly beaten, for the egg wash

good-quality jam and freshly whipped
  or clotted cream, to serve

Line a baking sheet with parchment paper.

In a bowl, sift together the flour and baking powder and stir in the sugar and salt.

Cut the butter into small pieces and rub through the dry ingredients with a pastry cutter, the back of a fork, or your fingers, or use a stand mixer or food processor—any which way you like to get a coarse, crumbly result. Pour the cream over the top and stir with a wooden spoon until just combined.

Turn the scone mixture out onto a lightly floured surface and press it together into a block. Let the dough rest for 5 minutes.

After it has rested, fold the dough in half, lifting and turning the dough over itself just the once. Press together and let it rest for another 5 minutes.

When ready, roll the dough out to 2.5cm (1 inch) thick and use a 6-cm (2½-inch) round cutter to stamp out even rounds, but try not to handle the dough too much.

Transfer the scones to the lined baking sheet, cover with plastic wrap and place the tray in the fridge or freezer for 10 to 20 minutes to rest. This will help the scones to keep their shapes while baking.

While the scones are in the freezer, preheat the oven to 200°C/390°F (180°C/355°F convection).

Brush the scones with the egg wash and bake for 18 to 25 minutes, depending on their size.

Remove from the oven and transfer to a wire rack to cool completely. To serve, split the scones in half, spread with jam and fill with cream.

Wild blackberry crumble tart

My older brother, Louis, always makes this tart in the summer. It is super-fast to put together and any leftovers are perfect for breakfast. The recipe was passed down to him from Norma Wells, a good baker and great tennis player. Louis is a fine cook and baker but, most of all, an accomplished forager. He makes this tart with wild huckleberries, a North American wild blueberry, which grow abundantly on the West Coast from Northern California to Canada. Bears especially love them. If you can find huckleberries, substitute them here. Now that I live in London I go to the Hackney Marshes to forage for wild blackberries in the hedgerows there in late summer. Finding these wild blackberries was one of the things that made my move to London bearable. I thought, if I could forage for wild blackberries, I could live here.

Makes one 20-cm (8-inch) tart, which cuts into 6 to 8 slices

FOR THE PASTRY

140g (1 cup) all-purpose flour

2 tablespoons sugar

115g (½ cup plus 2 tablespoons) unsalted butter, softened

1 tablespoon white vinegar

butter, for greasing the pan

FOR THE FILLING

100g (½ cup) sugar

2 tablespoons all-purpose flour

1 teaspoon ground cinnamon

a pinch of kosher salt

400g (3½ cups) fresh blackberries

Preheat the oven to 200°C/390°F (180°C/355°F convection). Butter a 20-cm (8-inch) tart pan.

Put all the pastry ingredients into a food processor and pulse briefly so that the mixture just comes together. Press all but 3 tablespoonfuls evenly into the prepared pan (reserve the remainder to crumble on top), and set aside.

Mix together the filling ingredients (except the berries). Spread three-quarters of this mixture over the base of the tart. Toss the blackberries with the remaining dry mixture and tip onto the tart. Crumble the reserved pastry on top and bake for about 40 minutes until bubbly and golden. Serve immediately. Anything left over can be eaten the next day. It's delicious cold.

Mandarin, ginger, and rye shards

Thin and crispy, these are just the thing to have with an afternoon cup of tea or coffee. They can also be crushed up and folded through just-churned ice cream or simply sprinkled on top of yogurt. The trick is to use a sharp knife and slice them as thinly as possible when the dough is very, very cold. Cut them too thickly, and you'll end up with jaw breakers.

Makes about 48 shards

250g (1 cup plus 1 tablespoon) unsalted butter

2 tablespoons malt extract

100g (¼ cup) golden syrup

250g (1½ cups) light muscovado sugar

100g (3½ ounces) whole almonds, coarsely chopped

150g (5 ounces) candied orange peel, chopped

175g (6 ounces) crystallized ginger, chopped

1 teaspoon kosher salt

1 teaspoon ground cinnamon

1½ teaspoons ground cloves

1½ teaspoons ground cardamom

1 teaspoon ground coriander

500g (3⅓ cups) whole grain rye flour

zest of 1 Mandarin orange

In a small heavy-bottomed pan, melt together the butter, malt extract, golden syrup, and muscovado sugar. Stir gently—not vigorously—to help dissolve all the ingredients.

Add the chopped almonds, candied peel, ginger, salt, and all the spices, and leave to cool completely. When the mixture has cooled, stir in the rye flour until well combined, then stir in the mandarin zest.

On a long board or worktop lined with parchment paper, press the dough into a slab roughly 10 by 30cm (4 by 12 inches). Cover with parchment paper and smooth the surface with a rolling pin. Then wrap the slab in plastic wrap over the parchment paper and freeze for 24 hours.

After removing the dough from the freezer, allow it to rest for 10 minutes. Meanwhile, preheat the oven to 180°C/355°F (160°C/320°F convection).

While the dough is still very cold and firm, with a sharp knife shave it into thin shards (aim for 1 to 2mm/¹⁄₁₆ inch thickness), and place on a parchment-lined baking sheet, with about 5mm (¼ inch) space between each slice (you can fit a lot of slices on a sheet).

Bake for about 8 to 10 minutes, or until the shards are dark and starting to firm up. They will continue to harden and crisp up as they cool. Be careful they don't burn, as they can quickly go from perfect to bitter and burnt. These keep well for up to 1 week in an airtight container.

Chewy ginger snaps

We make these at Christmas at Violet and pack them in sweet little cellophane bags then tie them up with string. After the holidays, if any are left over, they make a pretty awesome base for cheesecake, too. Crisp and spicy, they really hold their own against a creamy cheese or served alongside ice cream or sorbet. When using ground cloves, I am cautious with quantities because they can easily overpower a dish, although I would hate to ignore them altogether. Extra cardamom is lovely, less cinnamon would work too. A pinch of sweet paprika adds interest, and I sometimes add ground coriander seeds. Consider what you will be serving the cookies with, and experiment.

Makes 12 cookies

210g (1½ cups) all-purpose flour
1½ teaspoons ground cinnamon
1½ teaspoons ground ginger
⅛ teaspoon ground cloves
¼ teaspoon ground cardamom
⅛ teaspoon ground nutmeg
¼ teaspoon ground coriander (optional)

a pinch of paprika (optional)
1 teaspoon baking soda
125g (½ cup) unsalted butter, softened
100g (½ cup) dark brown sugar
100g (⅓ cup) molasses
1½ teaspoons boiling water
sugar, for dredging

Preheat the oven to 180°C/355°F (160°C/320°F convection). Line a baking sheet with parchment paper.

Measure all the dry ingredients (except for the brown sugar) into a bowl and whisk well.

In the bowl of a stand mixer, cream the butter, brown sugar, and molasses until light and fluffy. Add the boiling water, then the dry ingredients, and mix until combined.

Using an ice cream scoop or two dessert spoons, scoop up individual portions and shape into balls. Roll in sugar, then place on the lined baking sheet and flatten them slightly, using the underside of a glass or a measuring cup.

Bake for about 15 minutes, until the tops crack a little but the cookies are still soft. They will become crisper as they cool. These keep well for up to 2 weeks in an airtight container.

Summer spelt almond cake

This nutty light cake is perfect for scattering any summer fruits on top of. Some will sink in and some will rest on top. If you want a less sweet cake, you can leave out the rose water icing.

Makes one 23-cm (9-inch) cake, which cuts into 8 to 10 slices

FOR THE SPONGE

175g (¾ cup) butter, softened, plus more for greasing the pan

175g (1 cup) light brown sugar

2 eggs

¼ vanilla pod, seeds scraped out

125g (1 cup plus 1 tablespoon) ground almonds

175g (1¼ cups) whole grain spelt flour

2 teaspoons baking powder

¼ teaspoon salt

200g (2 cups) halved cherries, or whole raspberries or blueberries

200g (7 ounces) peaches or nectarines, sliced

2 tablespoons sugar, for sprinkling

rose petals, for scattering on top (optional)

FOR THE ICING (optional)

200g (1½ cups) confectioners' sugar

1 to 2 tablespoons rose water

Preheat the oven to 160°C/320°F (140°C/285°F convection). Butter a 23-cm (9-inch) cake pan and line with parchment paper.

First make the sponge. In the bowl of a stand mixer, cream the butter and sugar until light and very fluffy. Beat in the eggs one at a time, mixing well after each addition. Add the vanilla seeds (pop the scraped pod into your Vanilla Extract, see page 228). Add the almonds and mix to combine.

In another bowl, whisk together the flour, baking powder, and salt, then gently beat these dry ingredients into the creamed butter mixture. The mixture will be rather stiff, but that's okay.

Spread the cake batter into your prepared cake pan and smooth the top with an icing spatula or rubber spatula. Scatter the cherries (or raspberries or blueberries) over the batter, then press the slices of peach (or nectarine) down on top to get the fruit inside the cake batter a bit.

Sprinkle with the sugar and bake for about 60 to 70 minutes, until an inserted skewer comes out clean and the top of the cake springs back to the touch. Let the cake cool in its pan for about 15 minutes before turning it out onto a serving plate.

If using the icing, whisk the rose water into the confectioners' sugar until smooth and runny. Drizzle over the cooled cake. Scatter with garden rose petals if you have them. This is best eaten on the day you bake it.

Olive oil sweet wine cake

Sweet wines may not be to everyone's taste, but I think they are underrated. I actually prefer them at the start of a meal rather than at the end, as I feel that their sweet and rich nature is the perfect foil for salty charcuterie or raw oysters. Making sweeter wines is labor intensive and risky. Botrytis, or noble rot, is a mold that can either transform ripe grapes into a delicious potion or cause them to rot right on the vine and be lost completely. One summer evening, my friend Guillaume and I held a wine tasting at Violet with the young Italian winemaker Marco Sara. He brought me a beautiful sweet wine the day before so that I could use it to make this cake to eat after the event. I decided to try his very special wine in one of my favorite, not-very-sweet cakes. It worked beautifully. So buy a good sweet wine and drink it at the start of a meal, keeping a little back to use in this simple delicious cake.

TASTE. Sample the wine you intend to cook with. It's said that you should not cook with a wine you would not drink, but more to the point, I think you should understand the taste of the wine you are cooking with so it complements the flavors in your dish.

Makes one 23-cm (9-inch) cake, which serves 8 to 10

150g (⅔ cup) sweet white wine, such as Moscato d'Asti or Sauternes

1 tablespoon honey

zest of 1 small orange

50g (3 tablespoons) vegetable oil

150g (⅔ cup) mild olive oil

200g (1¼ cups plus 2 tablespoons) all-purpose flour

¼ teaspoon salt

1 teaspoon baking powder

4 eggs, separated

200g (1 cup) sugar

oil, for greasing the pan

whipped cream, for serving

berries, for serving

Preheat your oven to 170°C/340°F (150°C/300°F convection). Brush a deep 23-cm (9-inch) cake pan with oil and line the bottom with parchment paper.

In a small heavy-bottomed pan, reduce the wine over medium heat by two-thirds until you have 50g (¼ cup). You can roughly eyeball this, but do weigh it before you add it to the cake mixture. Take off the heat and then add the honey and orange zest. Set aside to cool.

Measure out the two oils into a jug and set aside. Measure the flour, salt, and baking powder into a bowl and whisk together, then set aside.

Separate the eggs, placing the yolks in one bowl and the whites in another. Take two more bowls and measure out 100g (½ cup) sugar into each bowl. Add the sugar from one bowl to the yolks and whisk together immediately

or it will become grainy. Use a stand mixer on high speed, if you have one, so that you can get the yolks pale and fluffy and forming ribbons. Lower the speed to medium and continue whisking as you slowly pour in the oils, as if forming a mayonnaise. Once all the oil is incorporated, turn up the speed for a minute or so. Gradually whisk in the reduced wine mixture.

Sift the flour mixture over the oil mixture and gently fold it together. Now in a clean bowl, whisk the egg whites with the remaining 100g (½ cup) sugar until they form soft peaks. Fold them gently into the yolk mixture and pour into your prepared cake pan. Smooth the top with an icing spatula or rubber spatula and bake the cake in the middle of the oven for 50 to 60 minutes, or until set and springy and an inserted skewer comes out clean.

Allow the cake to cool completely before turning it out of the pan. Serve with lightly whipped cream and berries. This cake is also delicious the following day.

Egg yolk chocolate chip cookies

Somewhere between crisp and gooey, and made with plenty of dark chocolate and just enough salt to bring out the flavor, for me this is the perfect chocolate chip cookie. Nearly everyone has their own recipe for chocolate chip cookies, but when taking a course run by French pastry chef Pierre Hermé in Paris in 2006, I learned the technique of using egg yolks to dramatically change the texture of a dish. Pierre made a cookie using egg yolks that was rich and delicious and had a beautiful texture. His cookies were fancier and more elaborate than mine, but I realized the same technique could be applied to the traditional chocolate chip cookie to good effect. It's also a great way for us to use up all the egg yolks we have left over at Violet after making hundreds of coconut macaroons every week.

NOTE. At Violet, we use an ice cream scoop to portion the cookies perfectly, but at home you can use two dessert spoons.

Makes 16 large cookies

250g (1 cup plus 1 tablespoon) unsalted butter, softened

200g (1 cup plus 2 tablespoons) light brown sugar

100g (½ cup) sugar

½ teaspoon vanilla

3 egg yolks (save the whites for the Coconut Macaroons on page 154)

325g (2⅓ cups) all-purpose flour

1¼ teaspoons kosher salt

¾ teaspoon baking soda

250g (1½ cups) dark chocolate chips or broken-up bar of your favorite chocolate

Line a small baking sheet or pan (one that will fit inside your freezer) with parchment paper.

Beat the butter and sugars in the bowl of a stand mixer until combined but not too creamy—you are not aiming for light and fluffy here, as that would make the cookies too cakey. Add the vanilla and the egg yolks and mix well.

In another bowl combine the flour, salt, and baking soda and whisk together well. Add this to the butter and egg mixture along with the chocolate, and mix until combined.

Scoop individual portions of cookie dough onto the lined baking sheet or pan. If using spoons, pat each portion into a little ball. Cover with plastic wrap and freeze for at least 1 hour, or up to a month. If you are pushed for time, or simply impatient, you can bake them right away, but the cookies will be slightly flatter and less even than the ones here.

When ready to bake, preheat your oven to 180°C/355°F (160°C/320°F convection). Line a large baking sheet with parchment paper and arrange the cookies evenly on the pan, leaving enough space between each one so they have room to expand during baking (when they will almost double in size). If you are baking from frozen, allow the cookies 5 to 10 minutes out of the freezer before placing in the oven.

Bake for 18 minutes, until the center of each cookie is slightly soft and underbaked, but the edges are crispy and golden. Remove from the oven and allow to cool on the tray for 10 minutes before serving. These cookies will keep for up to 5 days in an airtight container.

The Violet butterscotch blondie

The butterscotch blondie made its first appearance in my *Whoopie Pie* book, but I have since tweaked the recipe and I'm including the new version here. It's sweet, salty, gooey, and very moreish. This blondie is extremely popular at Violet and guys really love it, which is another plus. Make it for someone you want to do something nice for. You won't regret it.

Makes 12 blondies

250g (1 cup plus 1 tablespoon) unsalted butter, plus more for greasing the pan

2 eggs

300g (1¾ cups) light brown sugar

1½ teaspoons vanilla extract

240g (1¾ cups) all-purpose flour

1¼ teaspoons baking powder

1¼ teaspoons kosher salt

125g (4½ ounces) milk chocolate, broken into small pieces

75g (2½ ounces) caramel shards (page 238)

Preheat the oven to 160°C/320°F (140°C/285°F convection). Butter a 30 by 20-cm (12 by 8-inch) baking pan and line with parchment paper.

Gently melt the butter in a small, heavy-bottomed pan and set aside to cool slightly.

In a large bowl, whisk together the eggs, sugar, and vanilla until frothy, then whisk in the melted butter.

In a separate bowl, whisk together the flour, baking powder, and salt, and add to the egg and butter mixture along with the milk chocolate pieces. Mix until just combined.

Pour the mixture into your prepared baking pan and smooth the top with an icing spatula or rubber spatula. Sprinkle the caramel shards over the top and bake for 30 minutes. The center should be puffed and set but still a little gooey.

Leave to cool completely in the pan, then cut into 12 thick but smallish pieces. These keep well for up to 3 days in an airtight container.

Chocolate sandwich cookies

The key to making these is to use a really good, very dark cocoa powder. At Violet, we use Valrhona. It tastes really chocolatey and the color is almost black, which for me is almost the most important part of these little guys.

NOTE. It's best to use a piping bag with a round or star tip to fill these, but if you don't have one, you can use a teaspoon.

Makes about 36 sandwich cookies

FOR THE COOKIES
175g (¾ cup) unsalted butter, softened
250g (1¼ cups) sugar
¼ teaspoon kosher salt
1 egg
½ teaspoon vanilla extract

75g (¾ cup) cocoa powder
185g (1¼ cups) all-purpose flour
1¼ teaspoons baking powder

FOR THE FILLING
1 recipe for Salted Caramel (page 200)
    or Violet Icing (page 222)

Beat together the butter, sugar, and salt until smooth and creamy. A stand mixer is best for this, but you can do it by hand if your butter is at the right temperature. Add the egg and the vanilla and beat to combine well.

In another bowl, whisk together the cocoa, flour, and baking powder. Sift this over the creamed butter mixture, and mix just to combine. Be sure to scrape the bottom of the bowl.

Lay two large squares of parchment paper on your work surface and scrape half of the dough out of the bowl and onto the center of one parchment square. Repeat with the remaining dough. Using your hands, form each portion of dough into a log shape about 3cm (1¼ inches) in diameter. Working with one log at a time, take hold of one end of the paper and roll it up and over the dough, twisting the ends to seal the parcel (see page 146). Repeat with the other log. Place in the fridge to rest for at least 2 hours (or you can freeze the dough to use later. Just let it defrost for a few minutes before slicing).

When ready to bake, preheat the oven to 160°C/320°F (140°C/285°F convection). Line two baking sheets with parchment paper. Unwrap one log at a time and, using a sharp knife, slice the dough into about 72 neat 5mm (¼ inch) coins in total (you'll need an even number of slices). If the dough gets too soft halfway through the cutting, roll it back up in the paper and pop it into the fridge while you slice the other log.

Lay the disks out in tidy rows on the lined baking sheets, leaving a space of about 2 to 3cm (1 inch) between each one to allow them to spread during baking. Bake for 10 to 15 minutes, until the cookies are set and firm to the touch but not starting to burn—careful, this can happen quickly.

Once all the cookies are baked, let them cool completely. Meanwhile, you can get on with making the filling (page 200 or 222).

Turn half of the cooled cookies upside down. Using a piping bag with a round or star tip, or a teaspoon, pipe or spoon about 1 dessert spoon of buttercream in the center of each upturned cookie. Now top with the remaining cookies and press them down gently so that the filling comes up to the edges but does not squeeze out of the sides. Allow them to dry for about 15 minutes before serving or storing. These will keep for up to 6 days in an airtight container.

Continued

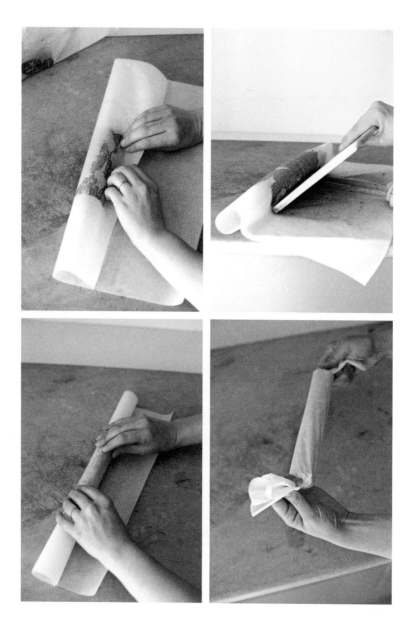

147

Pistachio, hazelnut, and raspberry friands

Friands are little French almond cakes, which we love at Violet because they are moist and tasty and also so easy to make. In this version, I substituted hazelnuts and pistachios for some of the almonds because I had a few left over that I wanted to use up. I really like the way these turned out, because the hazelnut has a lovely light flavor and the pistachio gives them a pretty pop of color. It is another recipe that we can have fun with at Violet, as the nutty base lends itself to a variety of seasonal fruit toppings. Here I've used raspberries, but you could use any berries you like, or slices of peaches, nectarines, plums, figs, or whatever.

Makes 12 to 16 friands

115g (½ cup) butter, melted,
   plus more or greasing the molds
90g (⅔ cup) all-purpose flour
¾ teaspoon baking powder
50g (7 tablespoons) ground almonds
40g (6 tablespoons) ground hazelnuts

40g (6 tablespoons) ground pistachios
190g (1⅓ cup) confectioners' sugar
5 egg whites, slightly whisked
2 teaspoons vanilla extract
200g (7 ounces; about 40 to 50)
   fresh raspberries
50g (1¾ cups) slivered pistachios
confectioners' sugar, for dusting

Preheat the oven to 160°C/320°F (140°C/285°F convection). Butter 12 to 16 friand molds or muffin cups.

Combine all the ingredients (except the raspberries and slivered pistachios) in the bowl of a food processor and process until foamy (about 1 minute).

Spoon the mixture into the molds, filling them to about three-quarters full, then top each mold with 2 or 3 raspberries and sprinkle with the slivered pistachios.

Bake for 15 to 20 minutes, until the tops of the cakes are springy to the touch.

Leave the cakes to cool slightly in their molds, then remove and dust with confectioners' sugar. They will keep well in an airtight container for a few days.

Kamut, vanilla, and chocolate chip cookies

Kamut flour is from the wheat family but, like spelt flour, it has a low gluten content. It has its own unique flavor with a denser texture than all-purpose flour. I think its subtle nuttiness goes very well with the floral notes of Tahitian vanilla and a good milk chocolate such as Valrhona or Green and Black's. I also love it with coconut palm sugar, for its tropical notes and less refined flavor. These cookies are best eaten warm, while the chocolate is still melted, with a glass of your favorite milk, be it whole, soy, or almond.

Makes about 12 large cookies

125g (½ cup) unsalted butter, softened

125g (4½ ounces) coconut palm sugar, grated if solid

½ teaspoon kosher salt

1 egg

½ plump Tahitian vanilla pod, seeds scraped out

180g (1½ cups) Kamut flour

¾ teaspoon baking powder

½ teaspoon xanthan gum

100g (3½ ounces) milk chocolate, broken into pieces

100g (3½ ounces) dark chocolate, broken into pieces

a pinch of flaky sea salt (e.g., Maldon), for sprinkling on top

Preheat the oven to 180°C/355°F (160°C/320°F convection). Line a baking sheet with parchment paper.

Using a stand mixer, beat together the softened butter and palm sugar until creamy and paler in color. You don't want the mixture to be as light and fluffy as you would for a cake, so don't beat it for too long. Add the half teaspoon of sea salt, the egg, and the vanilla seeds and mix again until smooth.

In a separate bowl, whisk together the flour, baking powder, and xanthan gum. Add the butter and vanilla mixture, then fold in the chocolate pieces.

Scoop or spoon 12 golf ball–sized portions onto the lined baking sheet, leaving enough space between each one to allow them to spread, then sprinkle each one with the salt.

Bake for 15 minutes until the cookies are a light golden color. Serve immediately or leave to cool and keep in an airtight container for up to a week.

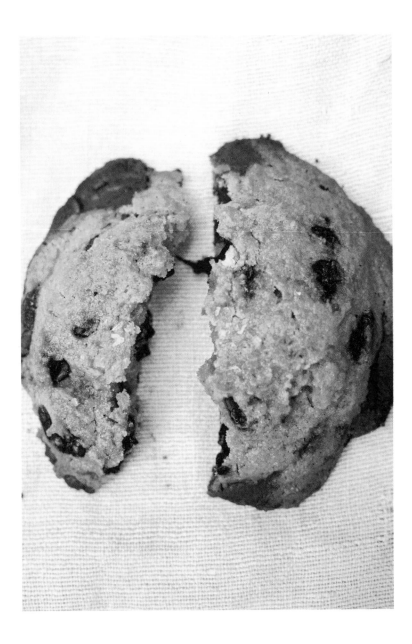

Rye chocolate brownies

The Violet brownie has seen many transformations since the early days of our market stall. An example of how texture and flavor are not mutually exclusive, a good brownie is all about richness and doneness, and when it's good, it transcends chocolate, elevating it to a whole new taste sensation. The inspiration for this brownie came from my friend and fellow baker Chad Robertson, who, in his *Tartine Book No. 3,* combined rye and chocolate flavors to make his Salted Chocolate–Rye Cookies. I'd been making brownies with spelt flour for over a year and thought they couldn't be bettered. But after reading Chad's book I decided to try making them with whole grain rye flour. The result was a chewy, rich, gooey, nutty chocolate treat. I immediately adjusted my recipe and haven't looked back.

Makes 12 brownies

150g (⅔ cup) unsalted butter,
  cut into small pieces, plus more
  for greasing the pan
300g (10½ ounces) dark chocolate
  (at least 60 to 70 percent cocoa
  solids), broken into pieces
50g (½ cup) cocoa powder
200g (1⅓ cups) whole grain rye flour

½ teaspoon baking powder
1 teaspoon salt
200g (1 cup) unrefined sugar
200g (1 cup plus 2 tablespoons)
  light brown sugar
200g (7 ounces) eggs (4 medium)
1 tablespoon vanilla extract
1 teaspoon flaky sea salt
  (e.g., Maldon), for sprinkling on top

Preheat the oven to 180°C/355°F (160°C/320°F convection). Butter a 20 by 30-cm (8 by 12-inch) baking pan and line with parchment paper.

In a heatproof bowl, melt together the butter and the chocolate over a pan of water that has been brought to a boil and then taken off the heat. Allow the mixture to rest, stirring occasionally as it melts.

In another bowl, whisk together the cocoa, rye flour, baking powder, and salt.

In the bowl of a stand mixer, whisk together the sugars, eggs, and vanilla until light and fluffy. Slowly add the melted chocolate, followed by the dry ingredients. Mix just enough to combine, then pour into the prepared baking pan. Smooth the top with an icing spatula or rubber spatula and sprinkle with a teaspoon or so of nice big flakes of sea salt.

Bake for 20 to 25 minutes, until the brownies are set but with a slight wobble. Leave to cool completely in the pan before cutting into 12 thick but smallish squares. These are best eaten on the day of baking.

Coconut macaroons

Coconut macaroons have been a staple at Violet since the first day of our market stall. When I was auditioning for a spot on Broadway Market back in 2005, my dear friend Dakota was visiting from California. Typical of Californians, she is always looking for ways to eat well and stay healthy, but she also loves a treat. At the time she was avoiding cakes made with flour and gluten and was obsessed with coconut macaroons. I wanted to make one that she would rate among the best and this was what I came up with. Now it's one of our most popular treats.

Makes 10 large macaroons

4 egg whites
250g (1¼ cups) sugar
¼ teaspoon kosher salt

1 tablespoon good honey
200g (1⅓ cups) unsweetened
    shredded coconut
½ teaspoon vanilla extract

Preheat the oven to 180°C/355°F (160°C/320°F convection). Line a baking sheet with parchment paper.

Measure out all the ingredients into a medium, heavy-bottomed pan and place over medium-low heat, stirring constantly. As the mixture starts to warm up, it will be easier to mix everything together. Reduce the heat to low and stir continuously until all the sugar has melted and the mixture starts to look like rice pudding.

Keep stirring until the mixture thickens and begins to dry out, keeping a careful watch to make sure it does not catch and scorch on the bottom.

Scoop individual portions of the mixture on to the lined baking sheet, leaving enough space between each one so they have room to expand. Bake for 15 to 20 minutes, until the macaroons are puffed and golden. Allow them to cool completely before serving or storing. These will keep well for up to 1 week in an airtight container.

Evening

In the first year of the Violet bakery on Wilton Way, I opened the upstairs dining room on a few occasions in the evening. I invited chef friends to come along and prepare a one-night-only supper for twenty-five people, cooked in our little kitchen in whatever style they wanted, and I would make the dessert. I really missed working in restaurants, and I had been hankering to make plated desserts again since I had left Chez Panisse. It was not only an opportunity to make very different things in the bakery, but also to collaborate and cook with other friends and professionals whom I really respected. The recipes in this chapter are the result of these collaborations.

I have also added tales and recipes from the events I participated in abroad with Alice Waters and the cooks of Chez Panisse. Just before I opened Violet bakery, I was busy with my stall and food styling, but had a much more flexible freelance schedule. I was invited to collaborate with Alice and cooks past and present from Chez Panisse on a few international projects. These dinners took place in Vienna, Davos, Berlin, and Washington, DC, and were always in the winter. Alice loves apple tarts, and so because of the time of year, the apple tart became the staple, served with some sort of ice cream. I developed a recipe for a light walnut praline ice cream when we all went to Davos, Switzerland, for the World Economic Forum in 2007 and have recorded it here.

Summer pudding

I like a combination of different-colored currants in my summer pudding, but you could use all red, as is traditional. I love the color that you get from black currants and the flavor from white. This pudding has a dated look, but I like that. The bread should be white sandwich bread from a bakery. Commercial sliced white bread has lots of additives to make it rise and bake quickly and it tends to get a bit slimy, so avoid it. Don't be tempted by brioche or sourdough either. You want a bread that is bland but has structure. A milk bread or *pain de mie* works well. Start the day before you want to serve the pudding.

NOTE. You will need a 1.5-liter (6-cup) pudding basin or bowl with a flat bottom.

Serves 6 to 8

200g (1¾ cups) black currants,
  stems removed

200g (1¾ cups) red currants,
  stems removed

100g (¾ cup plus 2 tablespoons) white
  currants (or more red currants),
  stems removed

150g (¾ cup) sugar

1 tablespoon fresh lemon juice

1 vanilla pod

500g (4⅓ cups) fresh raspberries

1 loaf (about 500g/18 ounces)
  day-old white bread, crusts removed,
  sliced into 1-cm (½-inch) slices

cold heavy cream, to serve

Line a sieve with cheesecloth or muslin and set it over a bowl.

Put the black currants, red currants, and white currants in a heavy-bottomed
pan along with the sugar and lemon juice. Cut the vanilla pod down the middle
and scrape the seeds into the saucepan, then add the empty pod. Cook over
low heat for 3 to 4 minutes, stirring gently until the sugar dissolves. The fruits
will release their juices, but don't let them cook for too long—you want to
keep the flavors bright. Remove the pan from the heat, fish out the vanilla pod,
and set it aside for rinsing and drying so you can add it to your Vanilla Extract
(page 228), or simply discard it. Stir in the raspberries and leave them
for 10 minutes to melt into the hot currants. Strain the juice from the fruits
through the lined sieve into the bowl. Reserve the fruits.

To assemble the pudding, cut one of the slices of bread into a rough circle
to fit in the bottom of the pudding basin and cut the other slices in half to fit
around the sides. Dunk the slices of bread into the strained juice and then lay
them in the pudding basin. You will need to do this quite quickly so the bread
doesn't soak up too much liquid and fall apart. Start with the circular base
piece, then lay the slices lengthwise, bottom to top, overlapping them slightly
to line the bowl completely. Press them down gently to fit them into place.
Spoon the fruit mixture into the bread-lined basin. Place the last slices of
bread on top to cover the fruit, then pour any remaining juice over the top.

Find a plate that fits just inside the rim of the basin. Cover the top of the
pudding loosely with plastic wrap and place the plate on top. Put a weight
on the plate to press the pudding down (a jar of jam or something else in your
fridge would work well), then place the pudding basin in a dish to catch any
juice that might seep out while it is pressed. Chill in the fridge overnight.

To serve, remove the plastic wrap, put a large plate face down on top of the
pudding and quickly flip the pudding over. Give a good shake and you should
feel the pudding release onto the plate. Serve with cold cream.

Rhubarb galette

We made this tart for the very first Violet supper on Wilton Way. With the opening of the bakery imminent, I was struggling with nerves, but luckily my dear friends Christopher Lee and Janet Hankinson from Chez Panisse were in London at the time doing some restaurant consulting. There were still a few details to iron out at the bakery, such as how to store all of our boxes and bags, and which things to hide and which to display in such a small space. There is a fine line between the beauty of seeing the ingredients and machines in an open kitchen and seeing clutter and mess. Janet stepped in at the last minute to help me organize the space and get things rolling, and she gave me the confidence I needed for the bakery's opening.

Serves 8

1 round unbaked pastry (see Alice
  Waters's Apple Galette, page 174)
600g (21 ounces) rhubarb
150g (¾ cup) sugar,
  plus more for sprinkling
2 tablespoons all-purpose flour,
  plus more for rolling

1 recipe frangipane (page 242)
3 tablespoons unsalted butter, melted

FOR THE GLAZE
150g (5 ounces) tops and tails from
  the rhubarb
100g (½ cup) sugar
A few angelica stalks and leaves
  (if you have it in your garden)

Preheat the oven to 200°C/390°F (180°C/355°F convection). Line a large flat baking sheet or pizza pan with parchment paper.

On a lightly floured surface, roll the pastry out into a large circle about 30cm (12 inches) in diameter. Slide the pastry onto the lined baking sheet, then cover and put back in the fridge or freezer to chill while you prepare the rhubarb.

Cut off and discard the rhubarb leaves, then trim off and reserve the ends of each stalk. Cut the rhubarb stalks into three or four pieces and then cut each piece lengthwise into 5-mm (¼-inch) strips. Toss the rhubarb pieces with the sugar and the flour.

Remove the pastry from the fridge and arrange a ring of rhubarb pieces around the perimeter of the pastry, leaving a border of about 4cm (1½ inches). Roll the edge of the pastry up over the rhubarb to make a decorative edge. Spread a little soft frangipane on the center of the pastry and pile the remaining rhubarb over this.

Brush the pastry with the melted butter and sprinkle with the remaining sugar. Bake in the center of the oven for about 45 minutes. After about 15 minutes, rotate the baking sheet and, using a spatula, push down the rhubarb to flatten it. Rotate again after 15 more minutes to ensure even baking.

Make the glaze by boiling the reserved bits of rhubarb (and a few angelica stalks and leaves) with the sugar and a splash of water until the fruit is soft. Strain the syrup into a bowl, then brush it over the baked galette. Serve with Plum Petal Ice Cream (below).

Plum petal ice cream

NOTE. You will need an ice cream maker for this recipe.

about a cupful of petals from a blossoming plum tree
350g (1½ cups) whole milk
175g (¾ cup plus 2 tablespoons) sugar
4 egg yolks
650g (2¾ cups) heavy cream, chilled
honey, to taste (optional)
a pinch of salt (optional)

Put the petals, milk, and sugar in a heavy-bottomed pan and heat until just beginning to bubble. This won't take too long, so while the milk is heating up, whisk the egg yolks in a bowl to break them up. Measure the cream into a large container or bowl and set aside.

When the milk is ready, temper the yolks by pouring a little of the warm milk into them, whisking as you go. Now pour the tempered yolks back into the remaining warm milk in the pan. Stirring constantly, heat until the mixture just starts to thicken at the bottom of the pan. You can test this by bringing the stirring spoon up out of the pan every so often to check it. Now pour the milk and yolk mixture into the cold cream and whisk together to prevent the custard from cooking any further. Cover and put in the fridge for at least 1 hour to cool.

Once the custard has cooled, pour it through a fine sieve to remove all the petals and any eggy bits.

TASTE. Taste the custard. It may be just right or it may need a drizzle of honey to bring out the heady flavor of the petals. A pinch of salt will also help.

Pour into your ice cream maker and churn for about 20 minutes, following the manufacturer's instructions. Freeze for 1 hour before serving. It will keep for 3 to 5 days in the freezer before it starts to get icy.

Rum babas

The cutest little buns in the world. Soaked in boozy syrup, these little guys steal my heart every time. I want to make these for every special occasion.

Makes 8 or 10 babas depending on the size of your molds

80ml (⅓ cup) milk

2 teaspoons dried yeast

2 teaspoons sugar

a pinch of sea salt

3 eggs

300g (2 cups plus 2 tablespoons) all-purpose flour

125g (½ cup) unsalted butter, cubed

50g (⅓ cup) currants

3 tablespoons of your favorite rum

butter, for greasing the molds

FOR THE SYRUP

800g (4 cups) sugar

800g (3⅓ cups) water

4 tablespoons golden syrup

1 Ceylon cinnamon stick

2 star anise

orange zest (in strips, not finely zested)

400g (1¾ cups) of your favorite rum

Grand Marnier or Cointreau, to taste

chilled cream or crème fraîche, to serve

Butter 12 dariole molds or 8 cups of a muffin pan. In a small pan, heat the milk briefly so it is warm to the touch. If it becomes too hot, let it cool a little before stirring in the yeast, sugar, and salt. Stir to dissolve them, then leave it to rest for 10 minutes as the yeast starts to activate.

Crack the eggs into a large mixing bowl and break them up with a fork or whisk. Add the yeast mixture to the eggs and whisk together well. Sprinkle half of the flour over this and use a wooden spoon to bring the dough together (it will be very wet). Cover with a tea towel or some plastic wrap and place in a warm spot in your home to rise for 1 hour.

Sprinkle the remaining flour over the dough and use your hands, or the dough hook on a stand mixer, to knead the dough in its bowl until it is soft and silky. Shape the dough roughly into a ball. Scatter the cubed butter over the ball of dough, then cover once again and, again, leave it to rise for 1 hour in the warm spot.

Meanwhile, prepare the currants. Warm the 3 tablespoons of rum in a small saucepan, watching the entire time. Make sure there is no rum on the outside of the pan as it can go up in flames! If this happens, don't worry, the alcohol will burn out eventually. Take the rum off the heat and add the currants. Cover the saucepan and let them soak until ready to use.

Continued

The dough should have risen considerably at this stage. Pour the soaked currants and any rum in the pan over the butter and dough. Use your hands or a stand mixer with a dough hook to mix everything together into a silky mass. This could take up to 10 minutes. As you work the dough, it will become less sticky. Don't be afraid that it's too soft, though. It should be of a thick, pouring consistency. Divide the dough among the buttered molds, filling them about two-thirds full. Cover and place in a warm spot until the dough reaches the tops of the molds, but now that the butter has been added, be careful that the dough does not get so warm (keep away from direct heat) that the butter melts out of it. This will alter the flavor and texture of the babas.

Meanwhile, preheat the oven to 200°C/390°F (180°C/355°F convection).

Bake the babas for 15 to 20 minutes, until the tops are golden. Remove from the oven and place on a wire rack to cool.

Now make the syrup. Place all the ingredients (except for the rum, Grand Marnier or Cointreau, if using, and the cream) in a medium pan over low heat and stir to dissolve. Turn up the heat and boil for 2 to 3 minutes. While the syrup is reducing, pop the babas out of their molds and place on a large platter. Take the syrup off the heat, add the rum and Grand Marnier or Cointreau, and pour the syrup into a large serving jug.

To serve, pour the cream into a nice jug (chill the jug ahead of time if you can). Pour the syrup over the babas, really dousing them with it. They will immediately soak it up. Divide them among your guests and pass round the cold cream.

Walnut praline ice cream

This is not a quick recipe, but it is rather simple. You will need to prep the ice cream base the night before to infuse the full flavor of the walnuts into the cream. You don't need an ice cream maker, just a good electric mixer. Serve alongside the Apple Galette on page 174, ideally while the tart is still warm.

Serves 6 to 8

FOR THE ICE CREAM BASE
100g (3½ ounces) walnuts
600g (2½ cups) heavy cream
½ teaspoon vanilla extract
100g (½ cup) sugar
4 tablespoons water
2 egg yolks

FOR THE WALNUT PRALINE
100g (3½ ounces) walnuts
100g (½ cup) sugar
4 tablespoons water
a pinch of salt

a little sugar, to taste (optional)
a little cream, to taste (optional)
a pinch of salt (optional)
nocino, brandy, or cognac,
    to taste (optional)

Start your prep the night before you wish to serve this ice cream.

Preheat your oven to 170°C/340°F (150°C/300°F convection). Line a baking sheet with parchment paper.

Spread the walnuts for both the ice cream base and the praline out on the lined baking sheet and place in the oven for 4 to 5 minutes, just until you start to smell them. You are not trying to toast them, but merely warm them to release their oils.

Measure the cream into a large jug. Separate out half of the walnuts and coarsely chop them, leaving the other walnuts on the tray. Drop the chopped walnuts into the cream, add the vanilla, and chill the mixture overnight.

The praline can also be made the night before. Place the sugar in a small, heavy-bottomed pan over medium heat along with the water and salt and stir to dissolve. Once the sugar has dissolved, stop stirring and turn the heat up to high. Cook until it turns a deep amber color and starts to smell like caramel. When the caramel is ready, pour it over the warmed walnuts on the baking sheet and leave it to cool and harden. Using a sharp knife, break the praline into bite-size chunks and store overnight in an airtight container or plastic freezer bag in the freezer.

Start to make the ice cream the next morning if possible so that it has ample time to freeze. Select a pretty enamel pie pan or shallow bowl that is big enough to hold the ice cream, and place it in the freezer to chill. Remove the cream from the fridge and strain through a fine sieve into a bowl to remove the walnuts. Discard the nuts. Whip the cold cream into soft billowy peaks and set aside.

In a small, heavy-bottomed pan, heat the sugar and water for the ice cream base and stir to dissolve. When the sugar has dissolved, stop stirring and cook the syrup for 3 minutes until thickened but not colored. Meanwhile, place your egg yolks in a bowl and whisk until they begin to get light and frothy. When the sugar syrup is ready, pour it into the yolks in a steady stream. Whisk by hand or with an electric mixer until the mixture is pale, very fluffy, and cool to the touch. Whisk half of the fluffy yolks with half of the whipped cream to combine, and then fold in the remaining whipped cream until just incorporated, followed by the remaining yolks. Sprinkle over the praline and fold it through.

TASTE. Take a small spoonful of the cream mixture and also a little of the praline to get the full impact of the flavor. Does the walnut flavor really come through? You will be freezing it later, which will dull the flavor, so it should be a little sweeter than you want the finished ice cream to taste. If it's not sweet enough, add half a teaspoon of sugar, stir, and then taste again. If it's too sweet, add a teaspoon of cream. Salt is always lovely with nutty desserts, but it can overpower the flavor if you are not careful. The salt in the praline may be sufficient, but if not, add another pinch. Vanilla can also overpower walnut's subtle flavor, so resist the temptation to add much more. If it still seems to be lacking balance, it might want a splash of alcohol. With walnuts, I would reach for nocino, if you have some. Nocino is made from green, unripe walnuts and is the perfect thing here. If you don't have any, then try a dark liquor like brandy or cognac. Fold it in, and taste again. When you are satisfied with the taste of the ice cream, it's ready to freeze.

Scoop the ice cream into the cold container and place back in the freezer for at least 4 hours before serving.

Alice Waters's apple galette

Alice Waters taught me that it's always best to present people with food that is simple and tastes delicious and that is made using the finest produce. This way, the ingredients won't need too much additional flavoring or fiddly preparation.

The apple galette, or tart, is a staple on the menu at the Chez Panisse Café in Berkeley, California, where everything is seasonal and sustainable, and it encompasses Alice's approach to cooking. Thin and buttery French-style pastry is topped with warm, almost caramelized slices of apple, then sprinkled with sugar and brushed with a glaze made from the apple peel. It is light and still welcome after a substantial meal, when you fancy just a little sweet bite. Of course, a good ice cream served alongside makes it perfect for a special occasion.

I am sharing my version of the recipe here, which I have tweaked slightly but which is otherwise hardly changed from the original. I have made this tart in an eighteenth-century game kitchen fueled only by fire, in Austria; in a hotel kitchen in the Swiss Alps reached by a funicular that features in Thomas Mann's *The Magic Mountain*; and in a kitchen in Berlin overlooking the Brandenburg Gate. Again, I had the honor of making this tart in Washington, DC, on the eve of the inauguration of the first black president of the United States in 2008. Most recently, I made it in the London kitchen of Sally Clarke to raise funds for Alice's pioneering Edible Schoolyard Project.

Choose your apples wisely. You want one that will hold its shape but still have a soft texture and lots of flavor after cooking. Good varieties in the UK are Discovery and Cox's Orange Pippin. Gloken from Switzerland is the best I have ever tasted (nicknamed the "Rockin' Gloken" by a few of us), and at Chez Panisse we always used the crisp, tart Sierra Beauty. Try different varieties from your local market until you find your favorite. If your only option is the supermarket, go for Granny Smith or Pink Lady.

Serves 8

FLAKY PASTRY

140g (1 cup) all-purpose flour, plus more for rolling

a pinch of salt

a pinch of sugar

85g (6 tablespoons) cold butter, cut into 1-cm (½-inch) pieces

2 to 3 tablespoons ice water

FOR THE GALETTE

4 to 5 apples

25g (2 tablespoons) unsalted butter, melted

100g (½ cup) sugar

FOR THE SAUCE

the peel and cores from the above apples

500g (2 cups) unfiltered apple juice

100g (½ cup) sugar

1 to 2 tablespoons Calvados or other apple brandy

Walnut Praline Ice Cream (page 170), to serve

To make the pastry, combine the flour, salt, and sugar in a bowl. Cut in the cold butter with a pastry cutter or the back of a fork, or use a stand mixer. Avoid overmixing, so that you end up with larger chunks of butter than you would think. This will make the pastry more flaky once baked. Drizzle in the water and bring it all together without working the dough. Shape into a ball and wrap in plastic wrap. Leave to rest in the fridge for about half an hour.

When the pastry has rested, remove it from the fridge and let it soften while you prepare the apples for the galette.

Peel, quarter, and core the apples. Save all of the peel and cores and put them into a small pan, then set aside to use in the sauce later. Cut each apple quarter into 3-mm (⅛-inch) slices, then take all of the small end pieces of apple and chop them coarsely with a few of the nicer slices to make about a handful of chopped apple. Set these aside. Don't worry about the apples browning because this will disappear once they are baked.

Preheat the oven to 200°C/390°F (180°C/355°F convection). Line a heavy-bottomed baking sheet with parchment paper.

On a lightly floured surface, roll the pastry out into a large circle about 30cm (12 inches) in diameter. Slide the pastry onto the lined baking sheet. Arrange a ring of apple slices around the perimeter of the pastry, leaving a border of about 4cm (1½ inches). Sprinkle the coarsely chopped apples in a thin layer inside the ring of apple slices. Over this, arrange the remaining apple slices in a pretty pattern so that they are overlapping and you don't see any of the pastry or chopped apples poking through underneath.

Roll the pastry edge up tightly over the ring of apples and brush with the melted butter, drizzling a little over the apples too. Sprinkle the apples with about half of the sugar. The other half is to generously sprinkle over the pastry edge, which will give it a nice crunch once baked. Place in the oven and bake for 45 to 60 minutes.

While the galette is in the oven, prepare the sauce. Add the apple juice and sugar to the pan of peel and cores and place over medium heat for 20 minutes, stirring occasionally. Strain the sauce into a jug, then pour it back into the pan and reduce the liquid for another 10 minutes before stirring in the apple brandy.

When the galette is golden and bubbly, remove it from the oven and transfer to a wire rack to cool.

Serve the galette with Walnut Praline Ice Cream and pour the appley sauce over the top.

Melon granita

We served this on one of the hottest days I can remember in London, in the upstairs dining room at Violet, for Joseph Trivelli's Irpinia peasant food feast. The menu was rustic and filling with all the flavors of this southern Italian cuisine. We began the meal with Joe's delicate handmade orecchiette and ended it with this sweet ice. If you have a melon baller, use it here. I remember discovering the baller as a child, and it still makes me smile to use one.

Serves 4 to 6

3 small melons (about 2.2kg/
 5 pounds total weight), such
 as cantaloupe or Charentais

3 to 6 tablespoons sugar

¼ teaspoon kosher salt

a drop of rose water or orange
 blossom water (optional,
 see taste note below)

Place a shallow pie dish or roasting pan in the freezer to chill.

Cut two of the melons in half, saving the third one for serving. Scoop out and discard the seeds, then scoop out the flesh, but avoid scraping too close to the rind, as the tough inner layer is not particularly flavorful. Puree the melon in a food processor and then strain through a fine sieve.

TASTE. Taste the melon now. How sweet is it? How strong is the flavor? Add the sugar a tablespoon at a time, tasting after each addition. Sweeten it to just a note higher than you want the finished granita to taste, as you will be freezing it later and this will dull the sweetness. Add a pinch of salt and taste again. (A drop of rose water or orange blossom water would be nice here, too, but I would avoid lemon or lime as citrus can overpower the sweet perfume of melon.)

Pour into your prepared frozen container and place straight back in the freezer for 30 minutes. Then, using a whisk, agitate the granita. Do this every 30 minutes until it looks like sparkling icy snow. This will take between 3 and 6 hours, depending on the temperature of your freezer.

When ready to serve, scoop out the flesh from the third melon (or use a melon baller). Serve the granita in chilled glasses, garnished with chunks or balls of fresh melon.

Cherry cobbler

We first made this very American cherry cobbler at Violet to use up leftover scone dough. We had a heap of just-pitted cherries and I tossed them in a little flour, sugar, vanilla seeds, and lemon zest and dotted the top with the scone pieces. One of my very first baking assistants, Echo, loved this cobbler. She spoke of its virtues every time the cherry season came around...and after it passed...and before it started again. I've included it in this chapter because our staff parties are a chance to share the best food with the crew who are too tired to eat it at other times. Echo's farewell party was a Mexican feast, and it only seemed fitting that I make her one of these cobblers for dessert.

Serves 8

FOR THE FILLING

3 tablespoons sugar

2 tablespoons all-purpose flour, plus more for rolling

1kg (2¼ pounds) fresh sweet cherries, pitted

1 vanilla pod, seeds scraped out

zest and juice of 1 lemon

butter, for greasing the baking dish

FOR THE TOPPING

210g (1½ cups) all-purpose flour

2 teaspoons baking powder

¼ teaspoon salt

85g (6 tablespoons) cold butter, cut into small pieces

175g (¾ cup) heavy cream, plus more for brushing on top

sugar, for sprinkling on top

cream, créme fraîche, or ice cream, to serve

Butter a 20 by 30-cm (8 by 12-inch) oval ceramic or enamel baking dish.

To make the filling, combine the sugar and flour in a large bowl and toss with the cherries, vanilla seeds, and the lemon zest and juice. Set aside to macerate.

To make the topping, combine the flour, baking powder, and salt in a bowl. Add the butter and mix it in with the back of a fork or your fingers until the size of peas. Drizzle in the cream and mix just until it comes together in a ball.

Preheat the oven to 190°C/375°F (170°C/340°F convection).

Turn the dough out on to a lightly floured surface and press it into a 2-cm (¾-inch) thick square. Then fold the dough over, press it out again, and repeat a couple of times. Allow the dough to rest for 10 minutes before rolling it out to a thickness of about 2cm (¾ inch). Use a round 6-cm (2½-inch) cutter to cut out 8 scones.

Place the unbaked scones, with their sides touching, on top of the cherry mixture. Brush the tops with the extra cream and sprinkle with sugar.

Bake for 40 to 45 minutes, until the tops are golden and the fruit is bubbling. Serve warm with thick cream, crème fraîche, or ice cream.

Fig leaf ice cream

Fig trees can be found in many back gardens in London and often overflow onto the street. Seldom do the figs turn into much. The fruit tends to stay underripe throughout the season, unless the fig tree has the good fortune to grow inside a walled garden that provides it with much-needed warmth. This suits me just fine, because I am mostly interested in those large green fragrant leaves. For a wedding rehearsal dinner for two of our most regular customers, Rick and Caroline, my friend, chef Joe Trivelli, prepared a wonderful Italian Irapinian menu and I made this ice cream with roasted fig leaves.

NOTE. You will need an ice cream maker for this recipe.

10 new spring fig leaves
350g (1½ cups) whole milk
175g (¾ cup plus 2 tablespoons) sugar
4 egg yolks
650g (2¾ cups) heavy cream

Preheat your broiler on high. Lay the fig leaves out flat on a baking sheet. Place the pan on the highest rack in your broiler and leave the door ajar. After a few minutes you will start to smell the wonderful heady aroma of the fig leaves warming up and then starting to singe under the flame. Let them take on a little bit of color before you take them out.

In a heavy-bottomed pan, warm the milk, sugar, and fig leaves until just beginning to bubble. This won't take too long, so while it's heating up, put your egg yolks into a bowl and whisk to break them up. Measure the cream into a large container or bowl and set aside.

When the milk is ready, temper the yolks by pouring a little of the milk into them, whisking as you go. Now pour the tempered yolks back into the remaining warm milk in the pan. Stirring continuously, heat until the mixture starts to thicken at the bottom of the pan, checking it now and again by bringing your stirring spoon up out of the pan. Pour the custard mixture into the cold cream and whisk well to prevent the custard from cooking any farther. Cover and put in the fridge for a least 1 hour to cool.

Once the ice cream base has cooled, pour it through a fine sieve to remove the leaves and any eggy bits. Pour into your ice cream maker and freeze according to the manufacturer's instructions. Freeze in the freezer for 1 hour before serving. This will keep for 3 to 4 days in the freezer before it starts to get icy.

Roasted black figs

If you can't find black figs, green figs are fine.

1 fig leaf (if available)
6 ripe black figs
a little sweet or light red wine
sugar, for sprinkling
Fig Leaf Ice Cream (page 180), to serve

Preheat the oven to 180°C/355°F (160°C/320°F convection).

If you have a lovely fresh fig leaf, place it in the bottom of a roasting pan that is just big enough to hold the figs. Cut the tough stems off the figs and discard, then cut the figs into quarters. Place the figs skin side down on top of the fig leaf or in the bottom of your roasting pan. Sprinkle the figs generously with wine and then lightly sprinkle with sugar.

Bake for about 20 to 25 minutes, until the figs are soft and starting to brown along the edges. Serve with Fig Leaf Ice Cream and drizzle with any juices from the bottom of the pan.

Quince ice cream

This is a great ice cream to make if you have some already-roasted quinces in your fridge. If you don't, you can of course still make it, but you will need to prepare the quinces the day before you want to serve the ice cream. I buy fresh quinces in the autumn, and I always buy an extra bagful to put into a bowl in my house because they look and smell so exotic. Quinces take a bit of prep, so I tend to roast a large batch and then use them in various recipes over the winter. They also make wonderful preserves to use throughout the year. I make this ice cream every year for Thanksgiving, which I always celebrate with my buddy Fanny Singer. We cook for two days and invite about 15 or 20 North Americans and Brits and embarrass everyone into declaring what they are thankful for.

NOTE. You will need an ice cream maker for this recipe.

Serves 4 to 6

150g (5 ounces) roasted quince (page 241)

50g (3 tablespoons) quince roasting liquid

2 large egg whites (save the yolks for the Buckwheat Butter Cookies on page 108)

100g (½ cup) sugar

1 teaspoon golden syrup

a pinch of salt

150g (¾ cup) whipping cream, chilled

1 heaped tablespoon plain yogurt

a little sugar, cream, lemon juice, or salt, to taste (optional)

Using an immersion blender or food processor, blend the poached quince with half of the poaching liquid until smooth. Add the remaining liquid and blend once more. Set aside.

Place the egg whites, sugar, golden syrup, and salt in a heatproof bowl. Put the bowl over a small pan of boiling water, whisking continuously until the sugar has dissolved and the mixture starts to become frothy and opaque (or, if you have a candy thermometer, use it to bring the mixture up to 75°C/165°F). Remove from the heat and transfer to the bowl of a stand mixer, then whisk until you have stiff peaks of meringue.

In a large clean bowl, whip the cold cream and yogurt to very soft peaks. Fold in the meringue just to combine, then fold in the quince puree.

TASTE. Does the ice cream mixture taste balanced? It should be a little sweeter than you want the finished ice cream to taste as you will be freezing it later and this will reduce the flavor. If it's not sweet enough, add half a teaspoon of sugar, then stir and taste again. If it's too sweet, add a teaspoon of cream. Is there enough acid? Because quince is not acidic, it may need a squeeze of lemon juice to tone down the warm, sweet flavors. Lastly, check for salt. There's a pinch of salt in the meringue, but another pinch might just bring the quince flavor to life. Remember, these are tiny adjustments that can make a big difference. Go slowly and add only a little at a time.

Pour the mixture into your ice cream maker and freeze according to the manufacturer's instructions. I tend to underchurn a little so as not to make the ice cream too icy.

Chocolate, prune, and whiskey cake

The recipe for this cake first appeared in the *Observer Food Monthly* Christmas special as my Prune and Armagnac Cake. Prunes and Armagnac are a classic French duo, and their affinity with chocolate is undeniable. One summer Damian and I were staying with our friends Tim and Darina in their cottage in West Cork, Ireland, and I decided to make this cake. There was no Armagnac in the kitchen, but there was some Irish whiskey. It was just the working man's whiskey, nothing too fine or peaty. The result was gooey, chocolatey, boozy, and sticky; it's more of a pudding than a cake.

Makes one 20 to 23-cm (8 to 9-inch) cake, which serves 6 to 8

125g (4½ ounces) pitted prunes

40g (3 tablespoons) Irish whiskey

240g (8½ ounces) dark chocolate (70 percent cocoa solids), chopped into small pieces

200g (¾ cup plus 2 tablespoons) unsalted butter, plus more for greasing the pan

5 eggs, separated

100g (½ cup) sugar

¼ teaspoon sea salt

150g (1⅓ cups) ground almonds

Soak the prunes in the whiskey. If you can do this the night before, all the better.

Preheat the oven to 180°C/355°F (160°C/320°F convection). Butter a 20 to 23-cm (8 to 9-inch) cake pan and line with baking paper.

Put the dark chocolate and butter in a heatproof bowl and place over a pan of barely simmering water. Make sure the water does not touch the bottom of the bowl or it may spoil the chocolate. Stir occasionally to emulsify the butter and chocolate. Once the chocolate has melted, take the pan off the heat to cool slightly but keep away from any drafts.

Put the whites and yolks into two separate bowls and, starting with the yolks, add half of the sugar and whisk to thicken. Fold the thickened yolks into the melted chocolate, and set aside. Chop the prunes into eighths and add to the chocolate mixture along with the ground almonds.

Beat the egg whites with the remaining sugar and the sea salt until soft peaks form. Fold into the chocolate mixture just until incorporated. Pour into the prepared cake pan and bake for 30 to 35 minutes. The cake will be slightly soft in the middle, but do not overbake it or the gooeyness will be lost.

Serve warm or at room temperature.

Coconut cream trifle cake

A *tres leches* cake is a Mexican favorite. In San Francisco, there are still a couple of Mexican bakeries that make it the good old-fashioned way, with fabulous over-the-top icing decorations, for *quinceañeras* (coming-of-age parties) and christenings. I make mine with a classic American chiffon cake, which is soaked with a blend of sweetened condensed milk and coconut milk, then filled with coconut milk pudding and topped with cream. This cake is best served stone cold, straight from the fridge. You will want to make it in a deep cake pan (measuring about 23 by 33 by 7cm/9 by 13 by 2¾ inches) so it's big enough to hold this pudding-like cake. I like to keep my coconut pudding looser and more runny than is usual, and so the cake is best served in bowls. It's a bit like a trifle, really. The presentation is casual, but that can be rather nice now and again. To save time, make the pudding the day before you want to serve the cake. You could also bake the sponge the day before if you want to get organized ahead of the big day.

Continued

Coconut cream trifle cake continued

Serves 8 to 10

FOR THE COCONUT PUDDING

200g (¾ cup plus 2 tablespoons) coconut milk

50g (¼ cup) sugar

¼ vanilla pod, seeds scraped out

40g (3 tablespoons) water

1 tablespoon cornstarch

1 tablespoon water, for dissolving the cornstarch

a pinch of salt

1 teaspoon white rum

FOR THE CHIFFON SPONGE

160g (1 cup plus 2 tablespoons) all-purpose flour

1 teaspoon baking powder

150g (¾ cup) sugar

½ teaspoon salt

65g (5 tablespoons) vegetable oil, plus extra for greasing the pan

6 egg yolks

65g (¼ cup) water

1 teaspoon vanilla extract

a few grates of nutmeg

5 egg whites

¼ teaspoon cream of tartar

FOR THE COCONUT SOAK

200g (¾ cup plus 2 tablespoons) full-fat coconut milk, well shaken

200g (⅔ cup) sweetened condensed milk

FOR THE WHIPPED CREAM TOPPING

1 liter (1 quart) whipping cream

50g (⅓ cup) shredded coconut, toasted or untoasted, for sprinkling on top

First, prepare the coconut pudding. Put the coconut milk, sugar, vanilla pod, and water into a saucepan. Place over moderate heat, stir to dissolve the sugar and then turn up the heat to high. In a separate small bowl, combine the cornstarch and water, then add to the pan along with the salt, and whisk until thick. This should take about 10 to 15 minutes. Once the pudding is ready, pour it into a heatproof container and leave to cool for about 20 minutes. After 20 minutes, remove the vanilla pod and add the rum. Press a piece of plastic wrap on the surface of the pudding. Leave to cool, then put in the fridge to chill for at least 4 hours so it sets into the consistency of a creamy pudding.

Preheat the oven to 150°C/300°F (130°C/265°F convection). Grease only the bottom of a rectangular cake pan (about 23 by 33 by 7cm/9 by 13 by 2¾ inches) with oil and cut a piece of parchment paper to fit the bottom. Do not grease the sides, as you want the cake to gently adhere to the sides of the pan so that it does not sink into itself as it cools.

To make the chiffon, sift the flour and baking powder together into a bowl, then whisk in half of the sugar and the salt, and set aside. In another bowl, whisk together the oil, egg yolks, water, vanilla, and nutmeg. Make a well in the center of the dry ingredients and gradually add the wet ones, whisking to form a paste and then a batter (much like a pancake batter).

Meanwhile, in the bowl of a stand mixer, whisk together the egg whites, the remaining sugar, and the cream of tartar. Whisk up into firm, meringue-like peaks. Stir a third of this into the chiffon batter and then gently fold in the rest of the whites. Pour into your prepared pan and bake until set, golden and springy to the touch. Leave to cool in the pan.

While the cake is cooling, prepare the coconut soak. Whisk the ingredients together, then pierce holes in the sponge with a skewer and drizzle the soak over the cake in its pan.

Spread the chilled pudding in a layer on top of the soaked sponge, pushing it into the corners with the back of a spoon or an icing spatula. Place the whole cake in the fridge.

Lightly whip the cream for the topping. Remove the cake from the fridge and cover with the lightly whipped cream, then sprinkle with the plain or toasted coconut. (If you do toast the coconut, make sure you let it cool completely before putting it on top of the cream.) Serve right away or chill until ready to serve.

TASTE. If you were pairing the chiffon cake with other fillings and icings, you could use lemon or orange zest instead of nutmeg in the sponge. I love the combination of vanilla, nutmeg, and coconut because they seem to harmonize with one another. But if you wanted to use this chiffon recipe with a lemon curd cake, then lemon zest would be a better flavor choice.

Chocolate sunken soufflé cake

I used to call this a flourless chocolate cake in the early days of my cake stall, and it was so funny to hear people ask for the "flavorless" chocolate cake; however, Chocolate Sunken Soufflé Cake describes it better. It's a soufflé, made rich with dark chocolate, and when baked just right is super-rich and gooey but then just melts in your mouth and actually feels quite light. These types of flourless cakes were really popular in restaurants in the 1980s and 1990s, but today people tend to add lots of nuts to their chocolate cakes. I love a nutty chocolate cake, but a pure chocolate cake is so lovely.

NOTE. You need to use an electric mixer to get the right volume with this cake.

Makes one 23-cm (9-inch) cake, which serves 8 to 10

150g (⅔ cup) unsalted butter, plus more for greasing the pan
180g (6½ ounces) dark chocolate (70 percent cocoa solids)
¼ teaspoon kosher salt
4 eggs
150g (¾ cup) sugar
cocoa powder, for dusting on top

Preheat the oven to 170°C/340°F (150°C/300°F convection). Butter a 23-cm (9-inch) springform cake pan and line with parchment paper.

Melt the butter and chocolate with the salt in a heatproof bowl set over a pan of barely simmering water. Stir occasionally but not vigorously. Once the butter and chocolate have melted, remove the pan from the heat but keep the mixture warm and resting over the pan of water until ready to use.

Separate the eggs, placing the yolks into the bowl of your stand mixer first. Add half of the sugar and whisk until the mixture forms pale and fluffy ribbons and has doubled in volume. Remove the bowl of melted chocolate from the pan of hot water and set it on your work surface. Fold the whisked yolks into the melted chocolate. They should be marbly and not fully incorporated.

Continued

Wash out the mixer bowl and dry it thoroughly, and now add the egg whites to it along with the remaining sugar. Whisk on a high speed until medium-soft peaks form. Do not overwhip. The consistency of the egg whites should resemble that of the yolk and chocolate mixture. Fold the whites into the chocolate until just mixed, then pour into your prepared pan.

Bake for 30 to 40 minutes, until the top of the cake is puffed and just starting to crack. The cake will still have a bit of a wobble and will be puffing out over the top of the pan. Place the pan on a wire cooling rack and coax any extra overflowing cake back into the pan. Allow to cool for a good 20 minutes, then remove the sides of the pan, peel off the paper, and slide the cake onto a nice serving plate. Dust with cocoa powder before serving.

Party party

I wouldn't be writing this book today if it weren't for the cupcake craze. The delicious fruity mini cupcakes that we made in a kaleidoscope of colors won us a lot of great press and many loyal fans. This both inspired me and helped me to grow my business. Now we love to hate the little sponge cakes that brought us so much joy and nostalgia just a few short years ago. But we are fickle creatures and always on the lookout for the next culinary craze. Doughnuts, cronuts, whoopie pies, macarons, cake pops, and meringues have all tried; however, none have managed to capture the hearts of us all like the cupcake did. Still the perfect balance of icing and cake, the Violet cupcake has to be included among the pages of this book.

We love to help you celebrate all those special occasions at Violet, with birthday cakes, wedding cakes, christening cakes, and the like. We bake fresh cakes daily to have in the case on display for the last-minute shopper, but much effort has also gone into the developing of bespoke cakes for events. However, simple and delicious cakes with minimal decoration have always been my favorites. I prefer the color to come from the ingredients (strawberries, caramel, citrus, grapes, quince, rhubarb) and the style to be casual and chic.

Chocolate devil's food cake

This keeps really well for a couple of days, so it is great for celebrations, as you can get the cake made early. Bake the night before you want to fill it, as this gives the crumb a chance to settle. Similarly, it's best to fill the cake and then chill it for a couple of hours before icing the top and sides. It's much easier to ice a cold cake than a warm, crumbly one. However, a warm fluffy cake with caramel icing melting into it is dreamy, so if that's what you're after, make cupcakes instead.

Makes one 20-cm (8-inch) cake or 24 cupcakes, serving 12

220g (1½ cups plus 1 tablespoon) all-purpose flour

100g (1 cup) cocoa powder

1 teaspoon kosher salt

2 teaspoons baking soda

1 teaspoon baking powder

450g (2¼ cups) sugar

2 eggs

1 teaspoon vanilla extract

200g (¾ cup plus 2 tablespoons) buttermilk or plain yogurt

100g (7 tablespoons) vegetable oil

225g (1 cup) hot water

Preheat the oven to 160°C/320°F (140°C/285°F convection). Butter and line a 20-cm (8-inch) cake pan with paper, or line two 12-cup muffin tins with paper liners.

Measure the dry ingredients, including the sugar, into a large mixing bowl and whisk with a balloon whisk to distribute the salt, baking soda, and baking powder evenly throughout the other dry ingredients.

In another bowl, whisk together the wet ingredients (except for the hot water). Once they are well whisked together, slowly whisk in the hot water.

Make a well in the center of the dry ingredients and pour in half of the wet mixture. Starting in the middle of the bowl, whisk in a clockwise, circular motion. Don't switch direction or you'll end up with lumps. Gradually add the remaining wet ingredients until you have a smooth, liquid batter.

If you are making a large cake, pour the batter into your pan right away and bake for 40 to 50 minutes until the top is springy to the touch and an inserted skewer comes out clean. If you are making cupcakes, scrape the batter into a container that will fit into your fridge and place a lid on top. Chill the batter for at least 1 hour. This will thicken it and make it easier to spoon into your cupcake liners. Bake the cupcakes for 18 to 20 minutes, until the tops are springy to the touch and an inserted skewer comes out clean.

Decorate the tops and sides of your cooled cake or cupcakes with Salted Caramel Icing (page 200) or Marshmallow Icing (page 222).

Salted caramel icing

I love making caramel ice cream and when I started making icings for my cakes to sell on my stall in Broadway Market, I decided to use the same approach by flavoring butter, rather than cream, in this instance. I devised ways of spinning different flavors into the butter, which also lent their color and texture to each icing.

Makes enough to ice and fill one
20-cm (8-inch) cake or 12 cupcakes

75g (¼ cup) Salted Caramel Sauce (page 237)

125g (½ cup) unsalted butter, softened

1 tablespoon plus 1 teaspoon whole milk

1 teaspoon vanilla extract

¼ teaspoon kosher salt

550 to 750g (3¼ to 5⅓ cups) confectioners' sugar, sifted

In the bowl of a stand mixer, beat together the salted caramel sauce and butter until smooth. Add all of the milk along with the vanilla, salt, and 250g (1¾ cups) of the confectioners' sugar. Cream together on a low speed for at least 3 minutes (set your timer). Gradually add more confectioners' sugar as needed, until you get the consistency you want, to make a spreadable and creamy icing that is as light as can be.

Fragola grape icing

Cupcakes made with this icing look so dark and sophisticated, yet when you take a bite it sends you straight back to your childhood. Purple Welch's grape juice and grape-flavored Hubba Bubba or Bubble Yum all had that sweet and sour balance that I love, and the color was awesome. For this icing, you will need to seek out the strawberry-flavored fragola grapes that come from Italy and appear briefly in the autumn. We sometimes use muscat grapes at Violet, but the color and flavor are totally different. Table grapes will simply not do.

Makes enough to fill and ice one 20-cm (8-inch) cake or 24 cupcakes

FOR THE FRAGOLA GRAPE PUREE

200g (7 ounces) fragola grapes

2 tablespoons water

2 tablespoons sugar

FOR THE ICING

100g (½ cup) fragola grape puree (see opposite)

1½ teaspoons milk

1½ tablespoons fresh lemon juice

190g (¾ cup plus 2 tablespoons) unsalted butter, softened

500 to 750g (3¼ to 5⅓ cups) confectioners' sugar

a pinch of salt

To make the grape puree, take the grapes off their stems and put in a small, heavy-bottomed pan with the water and sugar. Heat until the skins start to burst open, stirring to dissolve the sugar. Let the mixture cool slightly and then push the fruit through a sieve or, better still, use a food mill if you have one, to break down the skins and remove the seeds. Then blend in a food processor until smooth.

To make the icing, measure out 100g (½ cup) of grape puree into a bowl and stir in the milk and lemon juice. In the bowl of a stand mixer, beat the butter and 250g (1¾ cups) of the confectioners' sugar until smooth. Gradually add the grape puree, scraping the bottom of the bowl as needed. Add another 250g (1¾ cups) of confectioners' sugar and mix on a low speed for at least 3 minutes (set your timer). Add the salt, then gradually add more sugar as needed until the icing has a light, creamy texture. Taste for balance, and add more lemon juice or sugar as needed.

Grandma Ptak's red velvet cake

Grandma Ptak used to make this for me on every visit, whether at her house in Illinois or ours in California. I have a great photo of me baking this cake with her when I was about seven or eight, and you can see the empty bottles of food coloring littering the kitchen worktop. Grandma's kitchen was the center of everything. She had five sons, who loved her very much and also loved their food. Raising five hungry boys in the 1950s, she welcomed the conveniences that were being marketed to the modern housewife. She had every new appliance before anyone else and would send microwaves and food processors out to us in California. While my mom was baking whole wheat bread for us out of the *Tassajara Bread Book* and making sandwiches with homemade blackberry jam and natural peanut butter, Grandma was making the same sandwich with Skippy smooth peanut butter and grape jelly on sliced Wonder bread! Bless her. This is a version of her cake made with the ingredients we use at Violet.

NOTE. This sponge also makes great cupcakes—the amount below will make about 30.

Makes one 4-layer 15-cm (6-inch) cake or one 25-cm (10-inch) cake, serving 8 to 10

FOR THE SPONGE

600g (3 cups) sugar

1 teaspoon kosher salt

5 eggs

250g (1 cup plus 1 tablespoon) vegetable oil

5 tablespoons red food coloring

2 teaspoons vanilla extract

50g (½ cup) cocoa powder

560g (4 cups) all-purpose flour

100g (¾ cup plus 1 tablespoon) cornstarch

500g (2 cups) buttermilk or plain yogurt

2 teaspoons baking soda

2 tablespoons white vinegar

butter, for greasing the pan(s)

FOR THE ICING

1 recipe Cream Cheese Icing (page 217)

Preheat the oven to 150°C/300°F (130°C/265°F convection). Butter and line four 15-cm (6-inch) cake pans or one 25-cm (10-inch) cake pan with parchment paper. (If making cupcakes, line muffin pans with paper liners.)

In a large bowl, whisk together the sugar, salt, eggs, oil, red food coloring, and vanilla. Whisk well to help the sugar start to dissolve.

In another large bowl, sift together the cocoa powder, all-purpose flour, and cornstarch. (I recommend sifting here, so the cocoa gets mixed in well.)

Pour the buttermilk or yogurt into a jug. In a small bowl, combine the baking soda with the vinegar, then stir into the buttermilk.

Whisk half of the flour and cocoa mixture into the egg mixture, then mix in half of the buttermilk mixture. Add the remaining flour and cocoa mixture and mix well. Finally, add the remaining buttermilk mixture and mix until smooth.

Pour the mixture into your prepared cake pan(s). If making 15-cm (6-inch) cakes, bake for about 35 minutes or until the top is springy to the touch and an inserted skewer comes out clean. If making a 25-cm (10-inch) cake, bake for about 1 hour (and for cupcakes 20 minutes).

Ice the cake(s) with Cream Cheese Icing (page 217).

Coconut milk icing

This was the very first icing that I made for the first cupcakes I sold at my stall on Broadway Market. At the time I sold only coconut-flavored cupcakes because they were—and still are—the ones I like best. I love their texture and the sense of the exotic that they evoke. Perhaps that first cold winter in London had something to do with it, too. What's not to love about a snow-like cupcake that transports you to the tropics once you take a bite? The dash of rum that I add, along with a pinch of salt, enhances the coconut flavor.

Makes enough to fill and ice one 20-cm (8-inch) cake or 24 cupcakes

100g (⅓ cup plus 2 tablespoons) full-fat coconut milk, well shaken

1 tablespoon vanilla extract

1½ teaspoons white rum

190g (¾ cup plus 2 tablespoons) unsalted butter, softened

500 to 750g (3¼ to 5⅓ cups) confectioners' sugar

a pinch of salt

Measure out the coconut milk into a bowl and stir in the vanilla and rum.

In the bowl of a stand mixer, beat the butter and 250g (1¾ cups) of the confectioners' sugar until smooth. Gradually add the coconut milk mixture, scraping the bottom of the bowl as needed. Add another 250g (1¾ cups) of confectioners' sugar, and cream together on a low speed for at least 3 minutes (set your timer). Add the salt, then gradually add more sugar as needed until you get the consistency you want.

Hazelnut toffee cake

Hazelnuts and toffee are good companions, and the dates bring the whole thing together. The golden hue of this fruit cake reminds me of the falling leaves of autumn, and it's ideal for serving at Christmas. I've made the recipe for two small cakes partly because it is rich and also because the second one makes a lovely gift, wrapped in baking paper sealed with a snazzy sticker or patterned tape.

Makes two 18-cm (7-inch) cakes, serving 12 to 16

FOR THE SPONGE

350g (12 ounces) dates, pitted and chopped

150g (5 ounces) hazelnuts, toasted and chopped medium fine

3 eggs

1 teaspoon vanilla extract

50g (¼ cup) sugar

50g (¼ cup) brown sugar

200g (¾ cup plus 2 tablespoons) oil

140g (1 cup) all-purpose flour

1½ teaspoons baking powder

¼ teaspoon salt

100g (7 tablespoons) plain yogurt

butter, for greasing the pan

FOR THE TOFFEE TOPPING

50g (1½ ounces) toasted hazelnuts, skins sloughed off

50g (3 tablespoons) water

200g (1 cup) sugar

FOR THE ICING

4 tablespoons water

300g (1½ cups) confectioners' sugar

Brandy or cognac, to taste (optional)

Preheat the oven to 170°C/340°F (150°C/300°F convection). Butter two 18-cm (7-inch) cake pans and line with parchment paper.

For the sponge, combine the dates and the toasted nuts in a bowl.

Using a stand mixer, whisk together the eggs, vanilla, and sugars until light and fluffy. Continue to whisk as you slowly drizzle in the oil.

In another bowl, whisk together the flour, baking powder, and salt. Add this to the egg mixture and whisk for a few seconds, to combine. Add the yogurt and whisk to combine, then fold in the dates and hazelnuts.

Divide the mixture between your prepared pans and bake for about 35 to 45 minutes, until the cakes are baked through and set, but not dry. The tops of the cakes will not spring back as much as other cakes do because the dates make the mixture moist and dense in the best possible way. Leave the cakes to cool in their pans while you make the topping.

Line a baking sheet with parchment paper and spread your toasted hazelnuts on the tray. Place the tray on your worktop, near the stovetop. Have your icing ingredients nearby, as they will be needed as soon as the caramel is ready.

Put the 50g (3 tablespoons) of water in a small, heavy-bottomed pan and sprinkle in the sugar. Bring to the boil and just as the sugar starts to caramelize, watch it very closely, then as soon as it starts to burn, pour half of the hot caramel over the hazelnuts. Leave to cool and harden and then break the praline into shards.

To make the icing, add the 4 tablespoons of water to the remaining caramel in the pan. Pour the runny caramel from the pan into the confectioners' sugar and whisk to a smooth paste. Add more water or confectioners' sugar until it has the consistency of soft buttercream.

TASTE. Does the icing taste too sweet? It might need a splash of brandy or cognac to mellow it out. The cake itself is not too sweet, so it can handle a fairly sweet icing, but cutting it with a little booze can work well here.

To finish, spread the icing on the cooled cakes and top with the shards of praline.

Loganberry-vanilla birthday cake

Loganberries are amazing but not easy to find. They are a hybrid of blackberries and raspberries, resulting in the best of both. I used them here because I thought if more people asked for them, more shops might stock them and, in turn, more farmers might grow them. I get them from Jane Scotter at Fern Verrow at the Spa Terminus in Bermondsey, south London, on Saturdays in the early summer. Some of my friends grow their own, and a few cheffy friends pick their own on farms in Kent. However, if you have more pressing demands on your time, this recipe also works well with raspberries or blackberries. If you make it with blackberries, though, add a little more lemon juice, as blackberries lack the necessary acidity.

   This vanilla sponge can be made the day before you want to serve the cake, but the icing is best made on the day.

NOTE. You will need a piping bag with a large round tip for this recipe.

Makes one 20-cm (8-inch) layer cake or two 15-cm (6-inch) cakes, serving 10 to 12

125g (½ cup) unsalted butter, softened, plus more for greasing the pan

200g (1 cup) sugar

3 eggs

1 teaspoon vanilla extract

½ teaspoon salt

300g (2 cups plus 2 tablespoons) all-purpose flour

2 teaspoons baking powder

160g (⅔ cup) whole milk

1 recipe for Loganberry Icing (page 216)

6 tablespoons Loganberry and Geranium Jam (page 253) or raspberry jam

Preheat the oven to 150°C/300°F (130°C/265°F convection). Butter a deep 20 by 7.5-cm (8 by 3-inch) cake pan and line with parchment paper.

In the bowl of a stand mixer, cream the very soft butter with the sugar until almost white and fluffy. Gradually add the eggs, vanilla, and salt and mix until fully incorporated.

In a separate bowl, whisk together the flour and baking powder, then add half of it to the butter mixture until just combined. Add the milk and mix until combined.

Now mix in the remaining flour. Scrape the bottom of the bowl and mix once more. Pour the batter into your prepared pan and smooth the top with an icing spatula or rubber spatula.

Bake for about 50 to 60 minutes, until the top of the cake springs back to the touch. Allow the cake to cool for 15 to 20 minutes.

Continued

Remove the cake from its pan by running a small paring knife along the inside of the pan to release the cake. Wash and dry your cake pan well, then line with plastic wrap with plenty lapping over the sides and set aside.

Using a serrated bread knife (the longest one you have), score a horizontal line a third of the way up the side of the cake and then slowly cut through the cake, keeping your blade as steady and as flat as possible to get a good horizontal cut. Keeping the cake intact, make another incision two-thirds of the way up the cake, repeating the above process, so that you are left with three equal layers of sponge. Trim the top layer slightly if it is domed. Slide a tart pan base or cardboard disk between the bottom and middle layers of the cake, and lift off the top two layers on to a large plate.

Slide the bottom layer of sponge into the lined cake pan. Pipe a border of icing around the edges of the sponge. Don't worry if the icing touches the sides of the pan, as you are essentially creating a dam for the filling. Now add 3 tablespoons of jam, smoothing it over the sponge. Pipe a few stripes of icing over the jam. This acts as a glue to adhere one cake to another and it also creates delicious pockets of jam and icing between the layers.

Place the middle sponge on top and repeat the above process. Top with the third sponge, then pull up the sides of plastic wrap and wrap up the cake tightly. You may want to cover with another layer of plastic wrap to ensure it's airtight. Place in the fridge and chill for at least 2 hours or overnight. Leave any remaining icing at room temperature.

If you have left the cake to chill overnight, you may want to rewhip the icing. The icing will naturally deflate ever so slightly, and benefits from a second whipping.

Once you have taken the cake out of the fridge, remove it from its pan, set on a cake stand and peel off the plastic wrap. Use an icing spatula to ice the sides and top of the cake. Scatter a couple of berries over the top, and serve.

Loganberry icing

*Makes enough to fill and ice one
20-cm (8-inch) cake or 24 cupcakes*

120g (4 ounces) fresh loganberries,
  plus 2 berries for decoration

500g (3½ cups) confectioners'
  sugar, sifted, plus 2 tablespoons
  for the puree

1 tablespoon milk

190g (¾ cup plus 2 tablespoons)
  unsalted butter, softened

½ teaspoon kirsch

½ teaspoon fresh lemon juice

To make the buttercream icing, puree the 120g (4 ounces) loganberries with
the 2 tablespoons of confectioners' sugar until smooth, then strain through
a fine sieve to remove the seeds.

Transfer the loganberry puree to the bowl of a stand mixer. Add the
milk, butter, and 250g (1¾ cups) of confectioners' sugar and beat on a low
speed for 3 minutes (use a timer, as 3 minutes is longer than you think).
At this point the consistency should really have changed. Add another 250g
(1¾ cups) of confectioners' sugar and beat for another 3 minutes. You are
aiming for a creamy and light texture, but you don't want it airy and fluffy.
The buttercream should also hold its shape and not be droopy when the
paddle is pulled out.

Add the kirsch and lemon juice and mix well. If the mixture is too soft, add
more sugar a spoonful at a time, erring on the side of caution. The less sweet
the better, but the buttercream has to be able to hold its shape when you come
to assemble the Loganberry-Vanilla Birthday Cake (page 213) later. When it's
ready, put a large spoonful into a piping bag with a large round tip.

Cream cheese icing

Makes enough to ice four 15-cm (6-inch)
cakes or one 23 to 25-cm (9 to 10-inch) cake
or 24 cupcakes

200g (¾ cup plus 2 tablespoons) unsalted butter, softened
250g (1 cup) cream cheese
750g (5⅓ cups) confectioners' sugar, sifted
1½ teaspoons vanilla extract

In the bowl of a stand mixer, whip the butter until it is light and creamy. Add the cream cheese and beat well. Gradually add the confectioners' sugar and beat on a low speed for 3 minutes. Scrape down the bowl, then add the vanilla and beat for another 5 minutes.

The icing can be kept at room temperature for a couple of hours; otherwise store it in the fridge for up to one week. Before using, remove from the fridge and let it soften for about 20 minutes, then whip again for about 4 to 5 minutes.

NOTE. Use a timer; the beating will take longer than you realize.

Carrot cake

For some years I resisted adding carrot cake to the Violet repertoire.
I didn't understand its appeal. Yet nearly every day at Violet, an innocent,
unassuming customer would walk in, look around at the twenty or so
gorgeous cakes we offered and ask, "Do you do a carrot cake?" It became
obvious that the carrot cake filled a certain emotional void for many people.
I decided not to deny them, but to make a carrot cake that even I would love.

Makes one double-layer 23-cm (9-inch)
cake, serving 12, or 24 cupcakes

FOR THE SPONGE

250g (9 ounces) carrots, grated

100g (1¼ cups) unsweetened
  shredded coconut

100g (3½ ounces) pecans, lightly
  toasted and chopped fine

400g (1¾ cups) vegetable oil

1½ teaspoons vanilla extract

400g (2 cups) sugar

2 eggs

2 egg yolks, plus 4 egg whites

320g (2⅓ cups) all-purpose flour

1 teaspoon baking powder

1 teaspoon baking soda

2 teaspoons ground cinnamon

½ teaspoon salt

FOR THE ICING/FILLING

1 recipe Cream Cheese Icing (page 217)

Preheat your oven to 170°C/340°F (150°C/300°F convection). Butter two
23-cm (9-inch) cake pans and line with parchment paper, or line two 12-cup
muffin pans with paper liners.

In a large mixing bowl, combine the carrots, coconut, and pecans and set aside.

In the bowl of a stand mixer, whisk the vegetable oil, vanilla, 200g (1 cup)
of the sugar, the two whole eggs, and the egg yolks until foamy. Add to the
carrot mixture and fold together. Wash and thoroughly dry this bowl.

In another bowl, whisk together the flour, baking powder, baking soda, and
cinnamon and fold into the egg and carrot mixture until barely combined.

In your clean mixer bowl, whisk together the egg whites, salt, and the
remaining 200g (1 cup) of sugar until the mixture forms stiff peaks. Fold
this into the carrot mixture until just combined. Either divide the mixture
between the two cake pans, leveling the tops with a rubber spatula, or scoop
it into the cupcake liners, filling each liner half-full.

The whole cakes will take about 1 hour to bake and the cupcakes about
25 minutes. The cakes are ready when an inserted skewer comes out clean.

Use the Cream Cheese Icing recipe on page 217 to decorate the cupcakes
or to fill and ice the top and sides of the whole cakes—or you can just ice
the tops of each cake and sandwich them together.

Violet icing

Violets were my favorite flowers from a very young age. I loved the way they smelled, I loved the way they looked, and I loved the way that wild violets popped up in and around our backyard—so much so that they became my imaginary violet friends. My mom had this wonderful typewriter that typed in cursive script and as I told her the story of my little talking violets, she typed it up on red paper. When I moved to London and discovered a gorgeous French violet-scented syrup, I created this recipe to use it in.

Makes enough to fill and ice one 20-cm (8-inch) cake or 24 cupcakes

100g (7 tablespoons) whole milk

1 tablespoon violet syrup (Monin has one available in the US)

190g (¾ cup plus 2 tablespoons) unsalted butter, softened

500 to 750g (3¼ to 5⅓ cups) confectioners' sugar

1 teaspoon fresh lemon juice

Measure out the whole milk into a bowl and stir in the violet syrup.

In the bowl of an electric mixer, beat the butter and 250g (1¾ cups) of the confectioners' sugar until smooth. Gradually add the milk mixture, scraping the bottom of the bowl as needed. Add another 250g (1¾ cups) of confectioners' sugar and mix on low speed for at least 3 minutes (set your timer). Add the lemon juice and more sugar as needed until you get the right consistency.

Marshmallow icing

This stuff is out-of-control delicious. The recipe appeared in my *Whoopie Pie* book, but we use this icing so often at Violet that I had to include it here, too. If you don't have a candy thermometer, I recommend you buy one. They are relatively inexpensive and make life in the kitchen much easier.

Makes enough to ice 24 cupcakes

3 egg whites

450g (2¼ cups) sugar

120g (½ cup) water

1½ tablespoons golden syrup

a pinch of salt

1½ tablespoons vanilla extract

1 vanilla pod, seeds scraped out (optional)

Have your stand mixer with the whisk attachment at the ready.

Measure all the ingredients into the metal bowl of the stand mixer and place over a pan of boiling water (do not let the water touch the bottom of the bowl or it will cook the egg whites). Whisk continuously until the sugar dissolves and the mixture is very warm to the touch. If using a candy thermometer, whisk continuously for 2 minutes or until it reads 70° to 75°C (158° to 107°F), whichever comes first. Transfer the bowl to your mixer and whisk on high speed until nearly stiff peaks form.

Put the icing into a piping bag with a large round tip (or use a spoon) and pipe (or spoon) large blobs onto your cooled cake or cupcakes. Add edible decorations of your choice. At Halloween, we make little "ghost" cupcakes, using two edible silver balls for the eyes.

The Violet pantry

SALT. I like to use fine sea salt or kosher salt in my baking. You can also use good old table salt too, but it will make the recipes slightly saltier. The problem with substituting salts in recipes is that the different size of the grains or flakes can greatly affect the volume. Since salt is usually measured in spoons, it is difficult to be accurate. For example, one teaspoon of table salt weighs about 7g, while one teaspoon of flaked sea salt, such as Maldon, weighs roughly 4g, and one teaspoon of fine sea salt or kosher salt weighs about 6g. So obviously it is important to use the salt called for in the recipe, or adjust the amount accordingly.

EGGS. The organic and free-range eggs I use in the UK are classed as medium. Here, a medium egg (in its shell) weighs between 53g and 63g (1.9 to 2.2 ounces), with the white weighing 33 to 43g (1.1 to 1.5 ounces) and the yolk around 20g (0.7 ounces). This is about equivalent to a "large" egg in the US, which weighs (in its shell) about 57g to 63g, or 2 to 2.2 ounces. This is helpful to know if you have larger or smaller eggs and want to substitute them in your baking. As hens age, their eggs increase in size. There are other factors that contribute to egg size too, like the amount of light that hens are exposed to and how and what they are fed.

BUTTERMILK. When the recipes in this book call for buttermilk, I am referring to cultured buttermilk as opposed to fresh, or traditional, buttermilk, which is the milk left over after churning butter. This type of buttermilk is traditionally lower in fat because most of the fat is extracted during the churning process. Cultured buttermilk, on the other hand, is milk to which healthy bacteria have been introduced, whether naturally or by inoculation, such as when making yogurt. The bacteria makes the milk acidic, which aids the leavening process and also helps digestion. Yogurt can be used interchangeably with buttermilk in these recipes.

BAKING SODA. Where buttermilk or yogurt is included in a cake recipe, it will most likely be paired with baking soda, which is

alkaline. This cake batter can "hold" for a day or so in the fridge before being baked. When the cake batter is heated, the acid (in the buttermilk or yogurt) reacts with the alkali (in the baking soda) to release carbon dioxide gas, which is what makes your cakes rise. You need to achieve the right balance of acid and alkaline to get the correct rise, texture, and flavor from your baking. So, if you are out of buttermilk or yogurt, plain milk just won't do as a replacement. Without the acid in the recipe, the carbon dioxide reaction won't occur and the overly alkaline cake will taste soapy. And be aware that acidic ingredients such as buttermilk, yogurt, natural cocoa powder, vinegar, and ginger should be paired with baking soda, rather than baking powder, as the latter has added acid. (This knowledge really comes in handy when you are baking on a larger scale. At Violet, some of our mixtures need to hold for a day or two in the fridge so that we can bake them fresh while also saving time by making bigger batches of mixture to bake as and when needed—this is crucial for a small baking business!)

Baking powder is baking soda with cream of tartar added in. The tartar is acidic and reacts with the soda in the same way as acidic buttermilk or yogurt. Mixtures made with baking powder do not hold well in the fridge because the powder starts reacting as soon as it becomes wet. So it will act and then deflate if it is not baked within a relatively short period of time. Trace amounts of moisture and heat can cause baking powder to lose its effectiveness over time, so it is always prudent to check the expiration date on the label before you use it, especially if you don't bake very often.

COCOA POWDER. To come out right, the recipes in this book require a dark, alkalinized cocoa powder like Valrhona. Dark cocoas have gone through a chemical process of alkalinization, known as Dutch process, which makes them less bitter, darker, and more chocolaty in flavor.

A note about acid and alkaline:
You may have noticed that some recipes you try that contain cocoa end up tasting soapy. This soapy taste is a result of too much alkalinity. Older recipes (especially in the US) used cocoa that is "natural," and more acidic. The acidity in cocoa needed to

be balanced with an alkaline leavening ingredient such as baking soda. Now that we are using mostly newer alkalinized (dutched) cocoas, we need to adjust some of our older recipes by adding something acidic. This is where buttermilk, yogurt, and crème fraîche play a crucial role. They can be an added acid that helps to contribute to the texture, flavor, and rising ability in your baking. Ever have a cake sink? It can sometimes be attributed to this balance or lack thereof.

BUCKWHEAT FLOUR. Buckwheat flour is a gluten-free flour and, despite the name, it has no relation to wheat. It is very strong in flavor (unlike all-purpose flour, which has virtually no flavor) with nutty and earthy notes. I love buckwheat, but it does not go with everything and, because it has no gluten, you cannot simply substitute it in place of all-purpose flour in a recipe. I love it in pancakes, cookies, and pastry. It also works very well in buttery recipes such as the Buckwheat Butter Cookies (page 108).

Vanilla extract

We make our own vanilla extract at Violet, and it's easy for you to do this at home too. A scraped vanilla pod has lots of flavor (even after it has been steeped in something). It can be rinsed, dried, and then added to a sterilized jar and topped up with vodka. After a week it will have started to develop a fabulous flavor, which will of course improve over time, and can be used in any recipe that calls for vanilla extract. So each time you use a vanilla pod in a recipe, add the used pod to the jar and it will continue to strengthen the "brew." Keep topping up the jar with vodka, or have two bottles on the go, like we do at Violet, and use one while the other one is brewing.

Spices

Grinding your own spices will really change your baking. At Violet, we go through kilos of cinnamon, cardamom, cloves, and star anise each year. We buy wonderfully fresh spices from our natural foods wholesaler and, because we go through them so quickly, we don't grind our own. At home, however, I grind all my own spices, including star anise, cinnamon, cloves, nutmeg, mace, and so on. A small coffee grinder is great for the job. If your grinder has a residual coffee aroma, grind a soft piece of bread in it. The bread absorbs the coffee flavor and can then be discarded, leaving the grinder clean and ready to use for spices.

Quince jelly

This jelly has ranged from nearly translucent with a golden blushy tint to full-blown orange. It varies slightly every time I make it, partially due to the quinces' different varieties and partly due to how long I let it cook. It is a preserve that we serve at Violet with cheese toasties for that salty-sweet balance we all love. It would also make a nice change from cranberry sauce in the holidays.

1kg (2.2 pounds) quince
sugar
3 tablespoons apple cider vinegar

Rinse the quince and wipe them clean of any fuzz. Cut them into 2-cm (¾-inch) chunks (keeping the peel and core and all). Put them into a heavy-bottomed pot and cover with water. Simmer for an hour and a half to two hours. The quince should be soft, tender, and starting to darken in color.

Line a sieve with cheesecloth or muslin or use a jelly strainer suspended over a bowl to catch the juices, and pour the fruit through into it. Let this drain overnight.

The following day, discard the fruit and weigh the liquid. For every 450g (1 pound) of liquid, you will want to use 300g (1½ cups) of sugar. Add the sugar to the liquid, stir to dissolve, and bring to a boil. Add the vinegar and boil for 15 to 20 minutes or until it starts to thicken.

Pour into sterilized jars and seal according to the manufacturer's instructions, or store in the fridge for up to a month.

Candied citrus peel

Homemade candied citrus peel is far superior to the bland stuff you find in the shops, and once you have made it yourself, you will never go back to buying it. Make this in the winter when citrus fruits are at their best and then keep it in the fridge for all your baking needs. Any leftover peel can be soaked in brandy for the rest of the year, ready to be used in Christmas cakes and puddings.

4 grapefruit, or 6 oranges, or 12 clementines,
   preferably organic and definitely unwaxed
1kg (5 cups) sugar
500ml (2¼ cups) water
150g (¾ cup) sugar, for tossing

Wash the grapefruit, oranges, or clementines. Cut them in half and juice them. Reserve the juice for drinking or using in another recipe.

Place the juiced citrus shells in a pan and cover with cold water. Bring to a boil and cook for 10 minutes. Drain, then return the peel to the pan and cover with fresh cold water. Bring to a boil again, then drain. Repeat this blanching process a total of five times for grapefruit, three times for oranges, and twice for clementines. After the final blanching, test the tenderness of the peel by piercing it with the tip of a knife. If it still seems a little tough, blanch it again.

Drain the peel and let it cool to the touch. With a spoon, scrape away the soft pith. Then slice into 5-mm (¼-inch) strips.

Place the blanched and sliced peel, sugar, and water into a clean pan and stir to dissolve the sugar. Once it has dissolved, stop stirring and bring the syrup to a boil. Boil for about an hour and a half, until the syrup reduces and small bubbles form on top. The peel will become slightly translucent.

Remove the peel from the syrup with a slotted spoon or spider and lay out on a wire rack placed over a piece of parchment paper on a baking sheet to catch the drips. The next day, touch the peel to see if it is almost dry, but still tacky. If it is too moist, the sugar you toss it in will dissolve, but if it is too dry, the sugar will not adhere to the peel. When the peel is ready, toss in the sugar.

Store in an airtight container in the fridge for up to 6 months.

Candied angelica

I started growing angelica in my garden because I love the flowers
and the lush green foliage. I have always been intrigued by the bright
green candied angelica used as a decoration for Christmas cakes
and gingerbread houses, but also slightly scared of it. It turns out that
angelica is deliciously herbaceous and complex when all the flavor
hasn't been cooked out of it.

500g (17½ ounces) angelica stalks
  (300g/10½ ounces trimmed weight)
500g (2½ cups) sugar
250g (1 cup) water

Wash the stalks and cut into 8-cm (3-inch) lengths. Put them in a heavy-
bottomed pot and cover with water. Bring to a boil and then cook until
just tender. Drain the angelica, rinse with cold water, and drain again.
Scrape the outer skin from the older stalks; young tender stalks are fine
with their outer skin intact (think celery). Place everything in a heavy-
bottomed pot with the sugar and water. Leave overnight to macerate.

The second day, slowly bring to a simmer for about 20 to 30 minutes,
until the angelica becomes slightly transparent. Drain (reserve the syrup
for a cocktail) and spread out on a rack to dry. When they feel slightly
tacky and slightly drier, toss the pieces in sugar if you want, or simply
wrap the angelica in an airtight container in the fridge. They will keep
for up to three months.

Salted caramel sauce

This recipe is a little challenging at first, but once you trust yourself
and are willing to take the caramel to the brink with confidence, you
will have a killer trick up your sleeve. At Violet, we use this sauce in our
Salted Caramel Icing (page 200), but it's also delicious drizzled over ice
cream or warmed and poured over chocolate cake. *Mise en place* is really
important here so that you are set to go as soon as the caramel is ready.

Makes about 500g (2 cups)

150g (⅔ cup) heavy cream
½ vanilla pod
4 tablespoons water
250g (1¼ cups) sugar
2 tablespoons golden syrup
1 teaspoon lemon juice
¼ teaspoon fleur de sel
65g (4½ tablespoons) unsalted butter,
   cut into small pieces

Measure the cream into a large, heavy-bottomed pan. Split the vanilla
pod and scrape out the seeds. Add the pod and seeds to the cream.

Put the water, sugar, and golden syrup into another large, heavy-bottomed
pan. Have the other ingredients measured out and ready to go.

Begin by heating the cream and vanilla. Keep an eye on it as it can bubble
over quite easily. Meanwhile, start heating the water, sugar, and golden
syrup—don't stir it, but you can swirl the pan if necessary—all the while
keeping an eye on the vanilla cream. As soon as the cream starts to bubble
rapidly, turn the heat off.

Once the sugar mixture starts to color, give it a few swirls. You want the
sugar to turn golden brown and then almost black. When you see a wisp
of smoke starting to rise out of the pan, you know it's done. Take the sugar
off the heat and immediately whisk in the vanilla cream. Don't worry about
the vanilla pod at this point as it will continue to infuse flavor. Stir in the
lemon juice, salt, and butter, mixing until smooth. Allow the caramel to cool
completely, then remove the vanilla pod, transfer the caramel to a plastic
tub (with a tight-fitting lid), and put in the fridge to chill. Once the caramel
is chilled, it can be used in the Salted Caramel Icing on page 200. Caramel
keeps well for up to 2 weeks in the fridge and 3 months in the freezer.

Caramel shards

We use these shards in our Butterscotch Blondies (page 143,) but you could add them to almost any cake, cookie, or bar and, of course, they would be awesome in brownies. Any leftovers can be kept in a plastic container in the freezer for up to three months.

Makes enough for 24 blondies

2 tablespoons water
150g (¾ cup) sugar

Have a sheet of parchment paper ready on a heatproof surface. Measure the 2 tablespoons of water into a heavy-bottomed pan. Cover with the sugar and place over medium-low heat until the sugar starts to dissolve. Resist the temptation to stir the pan, as this can cause crystallization. Once the sugar starts to dissolve, turn up the heat to medium-high until the sugar is a dark golden brown.

Pour the caramel onto the parchment paper in a thin and even layer. Leave to cool, then use a sharp knife to chop into smallish shards. Be careful, as the caramel can be quite hard.

Use right away or store in a plastic bag or sealed container in the freezer. Do not store it in the fridge or it will soften, melt together, and become tacky.

Roasted quince

I always used to poach quince, but a few years ago I started roasting them. I love roasting fruit because it concentrates the flavor. Roasting also allows you to add lots of lovely aromatics like bay leaves, lemon, and vanilla, as I have here. You could also include orange, cardamom, cinnamon sticks, or cloves. You can use roasted quince for my ice cream recipe (page 184) or pureed and added to buttercream. It is delicious as a fruit option for the summer spelt cake (page 136) or on top of the almond-cornmeal muffins (page 48).

4 or 5 quince
300g (1½ cups) sugar
100g (7 tablespoons) water
200g (¾ cup) fresh lemon juice
zest of 2 lemons
2 or 3 bay leaves
1 vanilla bean

Preheat the oven to 180°C/355°F (160°C/320°F convection).

Peel and core the quince and cut them into wedges by cutting them in half from top to tail and then cutting each half into thirds. Spread the wedges out in a single layer in a large, heavy-bottomed gratin or roasting dish. Sprinkle with the sugar and cover with water and lemon juice. Add the zest, bay leaves, and vanilla bean. Cover tightly with foil and roast for about 25 to 35 minutes, or until a deep pinky orange and tender to the touch.

Store in an airtight container in the fridge for up to 1 month.

Frangipane

This makes a great filling base for most fruit tarts. It's different from the thick almond filling that you find in traditional French dessert tarts, which are mostly frangipane with a bit of fruit added. I prefer the emphasis to be on the delicious cooked fruit, with just a smear of this almond cream between it and the crisp pastry. You will inevitably have some frangipane left over, and at Violet we use it to make "jammy almond toasts." We spread one of our quick jams on some day-old bread and top with a generous amount of frangipane. Then we sprinkle with sliced almonds and bake in a hot oven for about 20 minutes. Frangipane keeps well in the fridge for up to 5 days.

2 tablespoons unsalted
   butter, softened

2 tablespoons sugar

50g (7 tablespoons)
   ground almonds

1 teaspoon kirsch (optional)

1 egg yolk

4 teaspoons heavy cream

In the bowl of a stand mixer, beat the butter and sugar until pale and creamy. Add the ground almonds and beat well. Add the kirsch, egg yolk, and cream and beat well. Use while still soft.

Quick jams

These jams are quick to make—which means you'll want to eat them quickly, too! The measures I've given are only a rough guide and you can easily adjust them according to how much fruit you are using. The idea is to have lovely fresh, compote-like jams that are less sweet than traditional jams and also easy to make without all the hassle of preserving (which I find a little boring).

Rhubarb and angelica jam

Angelica is a great pairing with tart rhubarb. It can downplay the tartness of the rhubarb without your having to add too much sugar.

Makes 2 large jars

500g (18 ounces) rhubarb
375g (1¾ cups plus 2 tablespoons) sugar
2 small angelica stalks
juice of 1 lemon
1 teaspoon Chartreuse (optional)

Slice the rhubarb into small pieces. Put them in a heavy-bottomed pot with half the sugar and leave to macerate for 1 hour.

Add all the remaining ingredients to the pot except the Chartreuse (don't forget the remaining sugar). Place over medium heat and bring to a boil slowly, stirring with a wooden spoon until the sugar has dissolved. Once it has dissolved, stop stirring and boil rapidly for 15 minutes. Add the Chartreuse and boil for a further 5 minutes.

The jam is ready when most of the rhubarb is nearly translucent and the consistency has thickened.

At this point you spoon the jam, including the angelica stalks, into warm sterilized jars and seal, or simply put the jam into a suitable container (with a tight-fitting lid) and keep in the fridge for daily use for up to a month.

Apricot and pineapple sage jam

My friend Harry Lester introduced me to pineapple sage when I first
moved to London. This herb grows really well in my rather shady garden.
It has pretty red flowers and the most beautiful pineapple fragrance.

Makes 2 large jars

500g (18 ounces) apricots
375g (1¾ cups plus 2 tablespoons) sugar
½ vanilla pod
juice of 1 lemon
a pinch of salt
a small bunch of pineapple sage leaves, torn

Cut the apricots in half, remove the pits, and cut the fruit into quarters.
Put the fruit into a bowl with half of the sugar, then stir to ensure each
piece of fruit is covered. Leave the fruit to macerate for 1 hour.

Put the macerated fruit into a heavy-bottomed pan. Split the vanilla pod and
scrape out the seeds. Stir in the remaining sugar and the vanilla seeds and
pod, then add the rest of the ingredients. Place over a medium heat and bring
to a boil slowly, stirring with a wooden spoon until the sugar has dissolved.
Once it has dissolved, stop stirring and boil rapidly for 15 minutes.

The jam is ready when most of the apricots are nearly translucent and the
consistency has thickened.

At this point you can spoon the jam (along with the vanilla pod) into warm,
sterilized jars and seal, or simply put the jam into a suitable container
(with a tight-fitting lid) and keep in the fridge for daily use for up to a month.

Peach and peach leaf jam

If you are lucky enough to have access to peach leaves, use them in your jam. They have an almond-scented quality that lends complexity to these juicy summer fruits. In the same way as we use the *noyaux* from apricots to enhance their flavor, so we use the leaves from the peach tree to give depth to this jam. If you don't have the leaves, this is still a wonderful jam. You could also add a single drop of almond extract if you like.

Makes 2 large jars

500g (18 ounces) peaches
400g (2 cups) sugar
juice of 1 lemon
a pinch of salt
a handful of peach leaves

Cut the peaches in half, keeping the skin on; remove the pits and quarter the fruit. Put them in a heavy-bottomed pot with half of the sugar and macerate for an hour.

Add all the remaining ingredients to the pot except the leaves (don't forget the remaining sugar) and place over medium heat, bringing slowly to a boil, stirring with a wooden spoon until the sugar has dissolved. Stop stirring once it has, and then boil rapidly for 30 minutes. Add the peach leaves and cook a further 15 minutes. The jam is ready when most of the peaches are nearly translucent and the consistency has thickened. Remove the leaves.

Pour into sterilized jars and seal, or simply put the jam into a suitable container (with a tight-fitting lid) and store in the fridge for up to a month.

Strawberry and lemon verbena jam

Lemon verbena smells lovely and fragrant if you are lucky enough to have it growing in your garden and it makes a very soothing tea. It is not readily available as a fresh herb in shops, so if you can't find it, you can use dried verbena, which is sold as a tea or herbal infusion.

Makes 2 large jars

500g (18 ounces) strawberries
450g (2¼ cups) sugar
10 lemon verbena leaves (or a handful of dried)
3 tablespoons fresh lemon juice

Wash and hull the strawberries. Cut them into quarters (or cut them smaller if the berries are very large).

Put 100g (3½ ounces) of the strawberries with 100g (½ cup) of the sugar into a heavy-bottomed pan. Place over medium heat and crush the berries with a potato masher, or similar, while warming them through.

Meanwhile, put 200g (1 cup) of the sugar in a food processor along with the lemon verbena. Pulse to break up the verbena.

Heat the oven to 140°C/285°F (120°C/250°F convection) and line a roasting pan with parchment paper. Put the remaining sugar and the lemon verbena sugar into the roasting pan and warm through in the oven.

Meanwhile, add the remaining strawberries to the mashed fruit in the pan. Bring to a bare simmer and add the warmed sugars. Stir until the sugar dissolves, then add the lemon juice. Turn up the heat and boil for 12 to 15 minutes.

Spoon the jam into warm, sterilized jars or a suitable container (with a tight-fitting lid). Store in the fridge for up to a month.

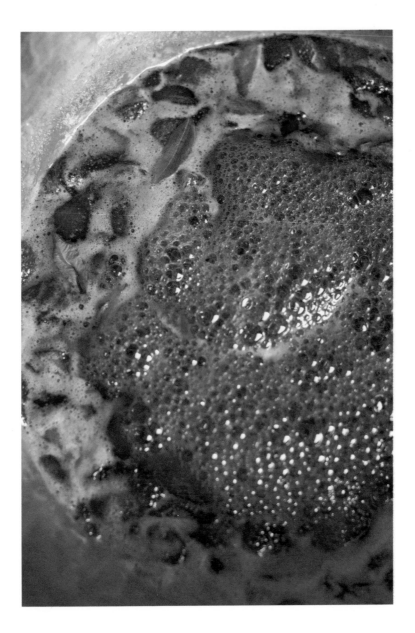

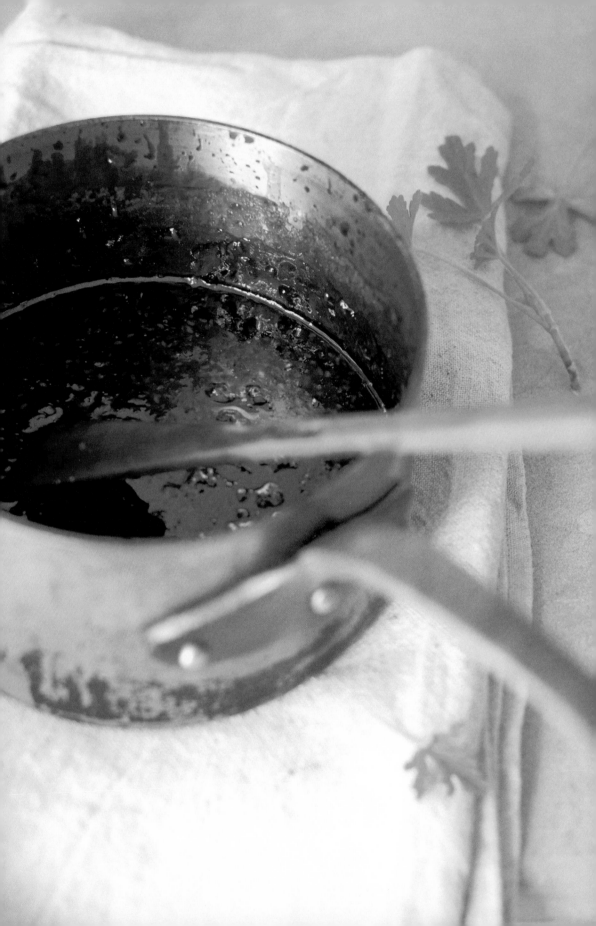

Loganberry and geranium jam

Dark berries are delicious with rose geranium, which is a lovely herb to use in baking. I strongly recommend you grow a rose geranium plant in a pot on your window ledge and use it in this jam. You can macerate the loganberries overnight if you want to, but this is not essential. I like to do this after a long afternoon of picking, when I am too tired to make the jam right away and have no space in my fridge to store the berries.

Makes 2 large jars

500g (18 ounces) loganberries (or raspberries or olallieberries)
500g (2½ cups) sugar
50 to 100g (¼ cup plus 2 tablespoons to ¾ cup plus 2 tablespoons)
 red currants, washed and stalks removed
4 rose geranium leaves, torn

Wash the loganberries and remove the stalks, then put into a bowl with 250g (1¼ cups) of the sugar. Leave to macerate, preferably overnight.

Put the loganberries and their macerating sugar into a heavy-bottomed pan and add the red currants.

Heat the oven to 140°C/285°F (120°C/250°F convection) and line a roasting pan with parchment paper. Place the remaining 250g (1¼ cups) of sugar in the roasting pan and warm in the oven.

Meanwhile, heat the macerated loganberries and the red currants over medium heat until just warm, then pound them lightly with a potato masher or similar. Add the warmed sugar and the rose geranium leaves and stir until the sugar dissolves, then turn up the heat and boil for 15 minutes.

Spoon the jam into warm sterilized jars or a suitable container with a tight-fitting lid. Store in the fridge for up to a month.

Plum and tonka jam

Tonka beans are one of my favorite spices. Their floral, tropical scent reminds me of the Mexican vanilla we used to enjoy as children. They can be used in the same way as nutmeg, grated into cakes and custards or, in this case, whole when making jam. You can find them online if your local shops don't stock them.

Makes 2 large jars

500g (18 ounces) red plums
375g (1¾ cups plus 2 tablespoons) sugar
½ vanilla pod
juice of 1 lemon
a pinch of salt
1 tonka bean, whole

Cut the plums in half, remove the pits, and cut the fruit into quarters. Put them into a bowl, cover with half the sugar and leave to macerate for 1 hour.

Split the vanilla pod and scrape out the seeds. Put the macerated fruit into a heavy-bottomed pan. Stir in the remaining sugar and the vanilla seeds and the pod, then add the rest of the ingredients. Place over medium heat and bring slowly to a boil, stirring with a wooden spoon until the sugar has dissolved. Once it has dissolved, stop stirring and boil rapidly for 15 minutes.

The jam is ready when most of the plums are nearly translucent and the consistency has thickened.

Pour the jam (along with the vanilla pod) into sterilized jars and seal, or simply put into a suitable container (with a tight-fitting lid) and store in the fridge for up to a month.

Notes on foraging

I started foraging as a very young child with my brother, mother, and father. At that time it was mostly berries, purslane, and of course sweet violets. The ephemeral scent of the sweet violet captured my imagination so much I named my business after it some thirty years later. As we got older we foraged for mushrooms and clams, delicacies with greater associated risks. My brother, Louis, is a great forager and took it a step further, diving off the coast of California in shark-infested waters for the prized abalone. Foraging is a bit of a sport. There is much competition over secret spots and bounty, and debate over whether or not foraged goods should be sold to restaurants and shops for fear that local stocks will be depleted. But for me, the most interesting aspect of foraging is that whether you live on the coast of California or in a tower block in east London, you can step outside and find growing edible plants and flowers that are delicious. Urban foraging can be a wonderful adventure. Amazing things grow in abandoned areas and along waterways. You are advised to use a guidebook for identification of wild plants as some are poisonous or even fatal. But we shouldn't fear our surroundings, we should embrace them. You are also obviously advised to ask if the plants you are foraging are overhanging from someone's garden.

Some of my most favorite foods to forage or pick from public areas in London are fig leaves, violets, blackberries, rose hips, sloes, mulberries, purslane, sweetpea blossoms, angelica, and the flowers and berries from the elder tree.

Index

acid, 39, 226–7

Acme Bread Company, 74

aerating, 30, 32

afternoon tea, recipes for, 102–55

agave: Chocolate oat agave
  cookies, 122–3

alcohol, 39

Alice Waters's apple galette, 173–75

alkalinity, 226–27

almonds
  Apricot and almond-
    cornmeal muffins, 48–49
  Frangipane, 242–43
  Nutty chocolate Barbados
    biscuits, 116–17
  Pistachio, hazelnut, and
    raspberry friands, 148–49
  Summer spelt almond
    cake, 136–37

Anchor and Hope, 19

angelica
  Candied angelica, 234–35
  Rhubarb and angelica jam, 245

apples
  Alice Waters's apple galette, 173–75
  Buckwheat, apple, and
    crème fraîche scones, 54–55

apricots
  Apricot and almond-
    cornmeal muffins, 48–49
  Apricot and pineapple
    sage jam, 246–47
  Apricot kernel upside-
    down cake, 110–13

Bacon and egg buttermilk
  biscuits, 58–59

baking powder, 226

baking soda, 224, 226

Banana buttermilk bread, 104–5

Barbados biscuits, 116–17

biscuits see cookies and biscuits

bitter taste, 38–39

Blueberry, spelt, and oat scones, 52–53

Bovine Bakery, 66

bread pudding, 74
  Braised fennel, olive, and caper
    bread pudding, 96–99
  Chocolate croissant bread
    pudding, 66–67
  Lacinato kale, leek, and ricotta
    bread pudding, 78–79

breakfast recipes, 42–73

Broadway Market, 22–24, 154,
  200, 207

brownies, Rye chocolate, 152–53

buckwheat flour, 227
  Buckwheat, apple, and crème
    fraîche scones, 54–55
  Buckwheat butter cookies, 108–9

buns
  Cinnamon buns 60–63
  Yellow peach crumb bun, 72–73

butter, 33, 40
  Buckwheat butter, cookies, 108–9
  Squash, brown butter, and sage
    quiche, 86–87

buttermilk, 224
  Bacon and egg buttermilk
    biscuits, 58–59
  Banana buttermilk bread, 104–5

butternut squash: Squash, brown
  butter and sage quiche, 86–87

cakes, 12, 25–29, 30, 102
  Apricot kernel upside-down
    cake, 110–13
  Banana buttermilk bread, 104–5
  Carrot cake, 218–19

Chocolate, prune, and whiskey
cake, 186–87
Chocolate devil's food
cake, 198–99
Chocolate sunken soufflé
cake, 192–95
Coconut cream trifle cake, 188–91
Coffee cardamom walnut
cakes, 106–7
Ginger molasses cake, 124–25
Grandma Ptak's red velvet
cake, 204–5
Hazelnut toffee cake, 208–9
Honey and rose water
madeleines, 126–27
Lemon drizzle loaf, 114–15
Loganberry-vanilla birthday
cake, 212–15
Olive oil sweet wine cake, 138–39
Pistachio, hazelnut, and
raspberry friands, 148–49
Red plum Victoria sponge, 118–19
Rye chocolate brownies, 152–53
Summer spelt almond cake, 136–37
Violet butterscotch blondie, 142–43
see also cupcakes; icings; muffins
cake pans, 33
capers: Braised fennel, olive, and
caper bread pudding, 96–99
caramel
Caramel shards, 238–39
Salted caramel, 36, 38
Salted caramel icing, 200–201
Salted caramel sauce, 236–37
cardamom: Coffee cardamom walnut
cakes, 106–7
Carrot cake, 218–19
cheddar
Cheddar and green onion toastie
with quince jelly, 76–77

Chipotle and cheddar corn
muffins, 88–89
cheese
Cheddar and green onion toastie
with quince jelly, 76–77
Chipotle and cheddar corn
muffins, 88–89
Comté and chutney toastie, 94–95
Cream cheese icing, 217
Ham, cheese, and leek
scones, 70–71
Lacinato kale, leek, and ricotta
bread pudding, 78–79
Mozzarella, rosemary, and new
potato tarts, 81, 83
Sour cream, chive, and feta
scones, 90–94
cherries
Cherry cobbler, 178–79
Quinoa, hazelnut, and cherry
granola, 44–45
Chez Panisse, 12, 15, 18, 30, 74, 156,
160, 174
Chipotle and cheddar corn
muffins, 88–89
chives: Sour cream, chive, and feta
scones, 90–94
chocolate
Chocolate, prune, and whiskey
cake, 186–87
Chocolate croissant bread
pudding, 66–67
Chocolate devil's food
cake, 198–99
Chocolate oat agave
cookies, 122–23
Chocolate sandwich
cookies, 144–47
Chocolate sunken soufflé
cake, 192–95

chocolate *(continued)*
  Egg yolk chocolate chip
    cookies, 140–41
  Kamut, vanilla, and chocolate
    chip cookies, 150–51
  Nutty chocolate Barbados
    biscuits, 116–17
  Rye chocolate brownies, 152–53
chutney: Comté and chutney
  toastie, 94–95
Cinnamon buns, 60–63
citrus peel *see* peel, citrus
Clarke, Sally, 174
cobbler, Cherry, 178–79
cocoa powder, 226–27
  Chocolate devil's food cake, 198–99
  Chocolate sandwich
    cookies, 144–47
  Nutty chocolate Barbados
    biscuits, 116–17
  Rye chocolate brownies, 152–53
coconut
  Coconut cream trifle cake, 188–91
  Coconut macaroons, 154–55
  Coconut milk icing, 206–7
  Sweet potato, coconut, date, and
    rye muffins, 56–57
coffee, 38
  Coffee cardamom walnut
    cakes, 106–7
Comté and chutney toastie, 94–95
cookies and biscuits, 30, 32, 102
  Bacon and egg buttermilk
    biscuits, 58–59
  Buckwheat butter
    cookies, 108–9
  Chewy ginger snaps, 134–35
  Chocolate oat agave
    cookies, 122–23
  Chocolate sandwich
    cookies, 144–47

Coconut macaroons, 154–55
  Egg yolk chocolate chip
    cookies, 140–41
  Kamut, vanilla, and chocolate
    chip cookies, 150–51
  Nutty chocolate Barbados
    biscuits, 116–17
  Oatmeal and candied peel
    cookies, 120–21
corn
  Chipotle and cheddar corn
    muffins, 88–89
  Sweet corn and roasted cherry
    tomato quiche, 100–101
cornmeal: Apricot and almond-
  cornmeal muffins, 48–49
Cream cheese icing, 217
Cream scones, 128–29
Crème fraîche: Buckwheat, apple, and
  crème fraîche scones, 54–55
croissants: Chocolate croissant
  bread pudding, 66–67
crumble
  Raspberry and star anise
    crumble muffins, 64–65
  Yellow peach crumb bun, 72–73
cupcakes, 29, 196
  using Carrot cake recipe, 219
  using Chocolate devil's food cake
    recipe, 199
  using Grandma Ptak's red velvet
    cake recipe, 205
  with Coconut milk icing, 206–7
  with Cream cheese icing, 217
  with Fragola grape
    icing, 202–3
  with Marshmallow icing, 222–23
  with Salted caramel icing, 200
  with Violet icing, 222
currants: Summer pudding, 158–59

dates: Sweet potato, coconut, date, and rye muffins, 56–57
desserts, 156–95
dry ingredients, 33

Earl Grey tea: Prune, oat, and spelt scones, 46–47
eggs, 224
    Bacon and egg buttermilk biscuits, 58–59
    Egg yolk chocolate chip cookies, 140–41
Essencia, 95
evening dinners, desserts for, 156–95

fennel: Braised fennel, olive, and caper bread pudding, 96–99
feta: Sour cream, chive, and feta scones, 90–94
Fig leaf ice cream, 180, 183
figs, Roasted black, 181, 183
food processor, 33
food styling, 19, 22
foraging, 256
Fragola grape icing, 202–3
Frangipane, 242–43
friands: Pistachio, hazelnut, and raspberry friands, 148–49

galette
    Alice Waters's apple galette, 173–75
    Rhubarb galette, 160–63
geranium: Loganberry and geranium jam, 252–53
ginger
    Chewy ginger snaps, 134–35
    Ginger molasses cake, 124–25
    Mandarin, ginger, and rye shards, 132–33

Strawberry, ginger, and poppy seed scones, 68–69
Grandma Ptak's red velvet cake, 204–5
granita, Melon, 176–77
granola: Quinoa, hazelnut, and cherry granola, 44–45
grapes: Fragola grape icing, 202–3
Guardian, 22, 40

Ham, cheese, and leek scones, 70–71
hazelnuts
    Quinoa, hazelnut, and cherry granola, 44–45
    Hazelnut toffee cake, 208–9
    Pistachio, hazelnut, and raspberry friands, 148–49
Hermé, Pierre, 140
Honey and rose water madeleines, 126–27
Hopkinson, Simon, 22

ice cream, 13–14
    Fig leaf ice cream, 180, 183
    Plum petal ice cream, 161
    Quince ice cream, 184–85
    Walnut praline ice cream, 170–72
icing
    Coconut milk icing, 206–7
    Cream cheese icing, 217
    Fragola grape icing, 202–3
    Loganberry icing, 216
    Marshmallow icing, 222–23
    Salted caramel icing, 200–201
    Violet icing, 222

jam, 12, 244–55
    Apricot and pineapple sage jam, 246–47

jam *(continued)*
    Loganberry and geranium
        jam, 252–53
    Peach and peach leaf
        jam, 248–49
    Plum and tonka jam, 254–55
    Red plum Victoria sponge, 118–19
    Rhubarb and angelica
        jam, 245
    Strawberry and lemon verbena
        jam, 250–51
    see also jelly
jelly
    Cheddar and green onion toastie
        with quince jelly, 76–77
    Quince jelly, 230–31

Kamut, vanilla, and chocolate chip
    cookies, 150–51

Lacinato kale, leek, and ricotta
    bread pudding, 78–79
Lee, Christopher, 160
leeks
    Ham, cheese, and leek
        scones, 70–71
    Lacinato kale, leek, and ricotta
        bread pudding, 78–79
lemon: Lemon drizzle loaf, 114–15
lemon juice, 39
lemon verbena: Strawberry and
    lemon verbena jam, 250–51
Lester, Harry, 246
loganberries
    Loganberry and geranium
        jam, 252–53
    Loganberry icing, 216
Loganberry-vanilla birthday
    cake, 212–15
lunchtime recipes, 74–101

macaroons, Coconut, 154–55
madeleines: Honey and rose water
    madeleines, 126–27
Mandarin, ginger and rye
    shards, 132–33
marjoram: Tomato and marjoram
    tarts, 80–82
Marshmallow icing, 222–23
Melon granita, 176–77
midday recipes, 74–101
mise en place, 30, 237
molasses: Ginger molasses
    cake, 124–25
morning recipes, 42–73
Moro, 19
Mozzarella, rosemary, and new
    potato tarts, 81, 83
muffins
    Apricot and almond-cornmeal
        muffins, 48–49
    Chipotle and cheddar corn
        muffins, 88–89
    Raspberry and star anise
        crumble muffins, 64–65
    Sweet potato, coconut, date, and
        rye muffins, 56–57

Neal's Yard Dairy, 77

oats
    Blueberry, spelt, and oat
        scones, 52–53
    Chocolate oat agave
        cookies, 122–23
    Oatmeal and candied peel
        cookies, 120–21
    Prune, oat, and spelt
        scones, 46–47
Olive oil sweet wine cake, 138–39
Oliver, Jamie, 19

olives: Braised fennel, olive, and
  caper bread pudding, 96–99
onions: Cheddar and green onion
  toastie with quince jelly, 76–77
Ottolenghi, Yotam, 22
Overnoy, Pierre, 95

parchment paper, 40
party food, 196–223
pastry
    Alice Waters's apple
      galette, 173–75
    Mozzarella, rosemary, and new
      potato tarts, 81, 83
    Rhubarb galette, 160–63
    Squash, brown butter, and sage
      quiche, 86–87
    Sweet corn and roasted cherry
      tomato quiche, 100–101
    Tomato and marjoram
      tarts, 80–82
    Wild blackberry crumble
      tart, 130–31
peaches
    Peach and peach leaf jam, 248–49
    Yellow peach crumb bun, 72–73
pecans: Nutty chocolate Barbados
  biscuits, 116–17
peel, citrus
    Candied citrus peel, 232–33
    Oatmeal and candied peel
      cookies, 120–21
pineapple sage: Apricot and
  pineapple sage jam, 246–47
Pistachio, hazelnut, and raspberry
  friands, 148–49
Plum petal ice cream, 161
plums
    Plum and tonka jam, 254–55
    Red plum Victoria sponge, 118–19

Poilâne Bakery, 74
Poilâne, Lionel, 74, 96
poppy seeds: Strawberry, ginger, and
  poppy seed scones, 68–69
potatoes: Mozzarella, rosemary, and
  new potato tarts, 81, 83
praline: Walnut praline
  ice cream, 170–72
prunes
    Chocolate, prune, and whiskey
      cake, 186–87
    Prune, oat, and spelt scones, 46–47
Ptak, Grandma, 204
    Grandma Ptak's red velvet
      cake, 204–5

quiches, 74
    Squash, brown butter, and sage
      quiche, 86–87
    Sweet corn and roasted cherry
      tomato quiche, 100–101
quince
    Cheddar and green onion toastie
      with quince jelly, 76–77
    Quince ice cream, 184–85
    Quince jelly, 230–31
    Roasted quince, 240–41
Quinoa, hazelnut, and cherry
  granola, 44–45

raspberries
    Apricot kernel upside-down
      cake, 110–13
    Pistachio, hazelnut, and
      raspberry friands, 148–49
    Raspberry and star anise
      crumble muffins, 64–65
rhubarb
    Rhubarb and angelica
      jam, 245

rhubarb *(continued)*
    Rhubarb galette, 160–63
ricotta: Lacinato kale, leek, and ricotta
  bread pudding, 78–79
River Café, The, 19
Robertson, Chad, 153
rosemary: Mozzarella, rosemary,
  and new potato tarts, 81, 83
rose water: Honey and rose water
  madeleines, 126–27
Rum babas, 164–67
rye
    Mandarin, ginger, and rye
      shards, 132–33
    Rye chocolate brownies, 152–53
    Sweet potato, coconut, date, and
      rye muffins, 56–57

sage
    Apricot and pineapple sage jam,
      246–47
    Squash, brown butter, and
      sage quiche, 86–87
St. John Bread and Wine
  restaurant, 46
St. John Restaurant, 19
salt, 36, 38, 39, 224
    Salted caramel, 36, 38
    Salted caramel icing, 200–201
    Salted caramel sauce, 236–37
Sara, Marco, 188
sauce, Salted caramel, 236–37
scales, kitchen, 33
scones, 102
    Blueberry, spelt, and oat
      scones, 52–53
    Buckwheat, apple, and crème
      fraîche scones, 54–55
    Cream scones, 128–29
    Ham, cheese, and leek scones,
      70–71

Prune, oat, and spelt scones, 46–47
Sour cream, chive, and
  feta scones, 90–94
Strawberry, ginger, and poppy
  seed scones, 68–69
Scotter, Jane, 212
shards
    Caramel shards, 238–39
    Mandarin, ginger, and rye
      shards, 132–33
Shere, Lindsey, 18
Singer, Fanny, 184
Sour cream, chive, and feta
  scones, 90–94
sour taste, 39
spelt
    Blueberry, spelt, and oat
      scones, 52–53
    Prune, oat, and spelt scones, 46–47
    Summer spelt almond cake,
      136–37
spices, 229
spring onions: Cheddar and green
  onion toastie with quince jelly, 76–77
Squash, brown butter, and sage
  quiche, 86–87
star anise: Raspberry and star anise
  crumble muffins, 64–65
strawberries
    Strawberry, ginger, and poppy
      seed scones, 68–69
    Strawberry and lemon verbena
      jam, 250–51
sugar, 28, 36, 40
Summer pudding, 158–59
Summer spelt almond cake, 136–37
Sweet potato, coconut, date, and rye
  muffins, 56–57
Tangren, Alan, 18

tarts
    Alice Waters's apple
        galette, 173–75
    Mozzarella, rosemary, and new
        potato tarts, 81, 83
    Rhubarb galette, 160–63
    Tomato and marjoram
        tarts, 80–82
    Wild blackberry crumble
        tart, 130–31
tasting notes, 36–39
teatime recipes, 102–55
toasties, 74
    Cheddar and green onion toastie
        with quince jelly, 76–77
    Comté and chutney toastie,
        94–95
toffee: Hazelnut toffee cake, 208–9
tomatoes
    Sweet corn and roasted cherry
        tomato quiche, 100–101
    Tomato and marjoram
        tarts, 80–82
tonka beans: Plum and tonka
    jam, 254–55
Trivelli, Joseph, 177, 180

vanilla, 38–39
    Kamut, vanilla, and chocolate
        chip cookies, 150–51
    Loganberry-vanilla birthday
        cake, 212–15
    Vanilla extract, 228
Victoria sponge, 118–19
Violet
    pantry, 224–55
    premises, 24–25
Violet butterscotch blondie, 142–43
Violet icing, 222

walnuts
    Coffee cardamom walnut
        cakes, 106–7
    Walnut praline ice cream, 170–72
Waters, Alice, 15, 18, 19, 156, 173
    Alice Waters's apple galette,
        173–75
weighing, 33
whiskey: Chocolate, prune, and
    whiskey cake, 186–87
Wild blackberry crumble tart, 130–31
Wilton Way, 24–25
wine: Olive oil and sweet wine
    cake, 138–39

yogurt
    with Blueberry, spelt, and oat
        scones, 52, 53
    with Quinoa, hazelnut, and
        cherry granola, 44

Thank you

Damian Thomas, Allan Jenkins, Alice Waters, Todd Selby, Jamie Oliver, Felix Neill, Kristin Perers, Kitty Cowles, Antony Topping, Jenny Wapner, Kate Bolen, Emma Campion, Aaron Wehner, Rosemary Davidson, Rowan Yapp, Simon Rhodes, Jan Bowmer, Elisabeth Ptak, Leila McAlister, Joseph Trivelli, Stevie Parle, Sylvia Farago, Jaime Perlman, Blanche Vaughan, Hugo de Ferranti, Tommi Miers, Fanny Singer, Mariah Neilson Blunk, Max Frommeld, Ido Yoshimoto, JB Blunk, Henry and Jemima Dimbleby, Colin Campbell, Sara Morris, Dan Matthews, Tim and Darina Allen, Rory O'Connell, Alice Cowling and Sunset Pictures, Ruth Warder, Sonia Morange, Alex Matthews, Maren Caruso, Claire Roberson, Lazuli Whitt, Whitman Shenk, Yolanda Porrata, Alex Porrata, Nicole Bartolini, The Schmidts, Harry Lester and Ali Johnson, Davo Cook, April Bloomfield, Amy Wolfie, Jessica Boncutter, Alan Tangren, David Lindsay, David Tanis, Ignacio Mattos, Charlie Hallowell, Beth Wells, Janet Hankinson, Christopher Lee, Russ Moore, Allison Hopelain, Malgosia Szemberg, Davia Nelson, James Lowe, Sophie Dening, Joe Woodhouse, Elaine Murzi, Peta O'Brien, Sarah Tildesley, Trina Papini, Sheri Evans, Ryan Roche, Gail and Robert Westbrook, Phoebe Von Reis, Rebecca and Carlos Porrata, Gayanne Enquist, Louis Ptak, Camille Jackson, Bob Horan, Shane and Leslie Grevin, Gene Ptak, Lindsey Shere, Chad Robertson, Liz Prueitt, Mary Canales, Giorgia McAllister, Angela Wilson, Clare Lattin, Carolyn "Cal" Marcus, Samantha Dixon, Anais Waag, April Carter, Sophie Garwood, Martha Hanks, Gilbert Pilgram, Mariana Kazarnovsky, Hrafnhildur Benediktsdóttir, Amani Al-Kidwa, Ella Thumin, Bridget Bobb, Sveta Graudt, Louise Cassidy, Julia Doherty, Oscar Humphreys, Rae Omara, Helena Goodrich, Rebecca Steel, Yasmin Gapper, Tabby Hanks, Beau Lamond, and Mese "Eddy" Kurt and Sahin "Hawk" Kurt from the Greenwood Road Costcutter.

"VIOLET"

HERITAGE APPLES
FROM SUFFOLK
50p SMALL
80p LARGE

BIRTHDAY
CANDLE

"VIOLET"

"VIOLET"

"VIOLET"

VIOLET
CUSTOM
THDA
NER
FRO   3.0

Published in the United States by Ten Speed Press,
an imprint of the Crown Publishing Group, a division
of Penguin Random House LLC, New York.
www.crownpublishing.com
www.tenspeed.com

Ten Speed Press and the Ten Speed Press colophon are
registered trademarks of Penguin Random House LLC.

Originally published in hardcover in Great Britain
by Square Peg, an imprint of Vintage, a division of
Penguin Random House Limited, London.

Library of Congress Cataloging-in-Publication Data
Ptak, Claire.
The Violet Bakery cookbook / Claire Ptak.—First edition.
    pages cm
  1. Desserts. 2. Baking. 3. Violet Bakery (London, England) I. Title.
TX773.P967 2015
  641.86—dc23
                    2014036768

Hardcover ISBN: 978-1-60774-671-3
eBook ISBN: 978-1-60774-672-0

Printed in China

Photography by Kristin Perers
Art Direction by Felix Neill
Food and Prop Styling by Claire Ptak

10 9 8 7 6 5 4 3 2 1

First American Edition